LEISURE AND TOURISM

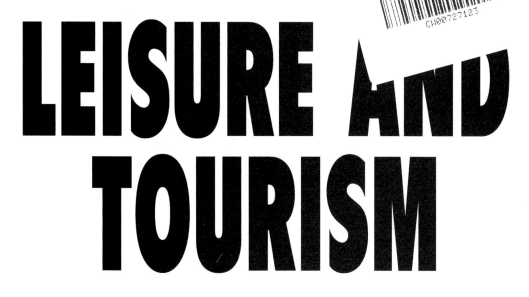

activities

FOUNDATION

MARION GOW

Hodder & Stoughton

A MEMBER OF THE HODDER HEADLINE GROUP

British Library Cataloguing in Publication Data
Gow, Marion, 1932–
   Leisure and tourism activities (Foundation)
   1. Leisure industry 2. Tourist trade 3. Leisure industry – Problems,
   exercises, etc. 4. Tourist trade – Problems, exercises, etc.
   I. Title
   338.4'791

ISBN 0 340 67404 0

First published 1997
Impression number   10 9 8 7 6 5 4 3 2 1
Year   1999 1998 1997

Typeset by Fakenham Photosetting Limited, Fakenham, Norfolk.
Printed in Great Britain for Hodder & Stoughton Educational, a division of Hodder
Headline Plc, 338 Euston Road, London NW1 3BH by Bath Press.

Contents

Providing service to customers

element 1.1

Investigate customer service needs

What is customer service?

There are leisure and tourism facilities which customers find adequate and others which make the customer feel relaxed and cared for. The difference is in the attitude of the staff.

All customers are important and should be treated as individuals. This will go a long way towards making the customer feel good and to want to use the facility again. Customers are the most important part of the business – without the customer, there would not be a business!

The customer's buying decisions are a result of the customer service received. Treating customers so that their expectations are met and taking extra care in doing this does not add to the cost of running the business. If staff keep customer needs in mind when doing their tasks, this adds value to the service being offered. Customers are valuable to leisure and tourism because without them there would be no need for the goods and services being offered, no business to be run and no jobs for the staff.

Customers respond well to staff who are interested in them.

The benefits of effective customer service

The customer who is happy with the service he or she receives will come back, will tell family, friends and acquaintances about the organisation so that they too may become customers. Staff can make the customer feel relaxed and well disposed by being helpful. People who come along to make enquiries and find alert and helpful staff will turn into customers. Everyone has their part to play.

The way in which an organisation's staff deal with the public decides if it has a good reputation or not. When *you* deal with a customer, *you* represent your organisation to the people you meet. Looking after the customer is a very important job. It has been found that customers who make a complaint and then have it put right are more loyal than ordinary customers who have never complained. If they receive good service, they tell other people about it and the firm adds to its good reputation.

Firms have goals to aim for. These are usually to make a profit, care for customers and obtain repeat business. Customers respond well to staff who are interested in them. If you know the names of your customers, use them. They will be pleased with the courtesy and service they receive and come again. They will turn into satisfied customers – and satisfied customers repeat the experience.

Job satisfaction comes from taking a pride in your work and showing a positive attitude to the job you are doing. One student who had a part-time job in a fast food takeaway felt rather bored with the job, so he decided to see how many customers he could make smile at him. To do this, he had to smile first. He was quite surprised to find how quickly the evening went and what a lot of pleasant customers he met! So be polite - smile at the customer. Know all about the service and products you are offering so that you can answer questions. You may become the staff expert on something in which you are interested and others will ask your opinion. To be good at your job brings the benefit of job satisfaction.

A benefit to yourself of providing good customer services is that the business is more likely to do well. This means that your job is more secure, pay increases and promotion are more likely and the business may be able to afford 'fringe benefits' for its staff (such as letting them have products or services at reduced prices). Job performance will improve, relationships with other members of staff will be better and the work will be done more efficiently. People working together accomplish more than individuals working alone. Learning as much as possible about the organisation, its products and services and your own job in it will help you to care more about your work - and about your customers.

The benefit of providing good customer service to the customer is that the occasion is turned into a very pleasant one. We all recognise when buying something, when we are being a nuisance to the sales assistants or whether they are pleased to help us! If the experience is one which the customer does not like, it will not be repeated. Customers should receive quality service along with the goods which they buy.

🏃 🏃 🏃 🏃 🏃 **ACTIVITY 1** 🏃 🏃 🏃 🏃 🏃

Work in small groups of between 2 and 4 people. Each person should describe to the others a situation where:

a they received poor customer service

b they received good customer service

From the descriptions, choose three things which staff should remember when dealing with customers – to make them feel that the organisation has a good reputation, that the staff care and that customers will return. Write your answer in full sentences.

Increased customer satisfaction, repeat business and a firm which has a good reputation means that the firm will continue in business, will make a profit and will need to keep its work-force. It does not cost anything to have staff who offer help and advice, who are pleasant to talk to and who can give correct information. Politeness costs nothing - but it can make all the difference to a business and its customers!

Customer safety and security

Customer safety is very important. New staff should be given training and checks should be carried out to assess whether there are any risks and what should be changed or improved. Maintenance should be carried out regularly, safety notices and fire exits should be clearly visible and safety rules should be kept. If customers are taking part in a sport where there are risks, they should be wearing the appropriate safety clothing and headgear. Riders and climbers should wear hats, people using water facilities should wear life-jackets. There should be proper supervision, especially of children. Protective clothing should be worn when fell walking or mountain climbing and customers should feel safe and secure when taking part.

ACTIVITY 2

Write out the following sentences, filling in the missing word(s).

1 The difference in a facility which customers find adequate and one which makes them feel cared for is the _____ of the staff.

2 There would be no jobs available in leisure and tourism organisations if there were no _____ to serve.

3 People who make enquiries and find _____ staff, may turn into customers.

4 Firms have as their goals: to make a profit, to care for customers and to obtain _____ _____.

5 Job satisfaction comes from taking a _____ in your work.

6 If you provide good customer service so that the business does well, your job is more _____.

Effective customer service

Meeting customers' needs

Meeting customers' needs is a very important part of customer service. Those customers who contact an organisation for help, advice and information will gain a lasting impression of that company from the person they first meet. It is important that all receptionists, telephonists and sales staff understand how important their work is.

Help should be given, but customers should not be made to feel under pressure to buy. Some customers do not know exactly what they want: for example, a leisure centre may have a variety of sports activities for the customer to choose from. Customers may not know exactly what equipment they are looking for and expect the assistant to help them to decide. Staff need knowledge in order to give help, advice and information so that the customer can make a choice. The information should also include the price of the product or service, with all the 'extras' included. It may annoy a customer if the price was altered after a decision had been made.

The strengths of the product or service should also be mentioned when giving information. The following list is basic and may be adapted to suit the circumstances when giving information. Staff may mention:

- price
- quality
- reliability
- convenience
- health-giving benefits
- after-sales service
- speedy delivery of service.

Ensuring customer health and safety

To ensure health and safety, the servicing of machinery and equipment used must be done regularly and recorded. In a large organisation, this information may be held on a database. Health and safety regulations must always be followed. Customers must feel safe when taking part in an activity and staff should check that they are using the correct gear. Boots, helmets, life-jackets and safety harnesses should be worn where this is appropriate. Supervision should be by qualified staff so that the customer feels secure.

Customers will be impressed with the care and efficiency of the organisation if the physical environment is free from hazards and if the equipment and supplies which are needed by

Servicing of machinery and equipment must be done on a regular basis.

customers are in place. The Health and Safety at Work Act gives information on safety and includes the following information.

Employers have the following duties:

1 They must provide and maintain plant and work systems which are, so far as is reasonably practicable, safe and without risks to health.

2 This also applies to the use, handling, storage and transport of articles and substances.

3 They must provide employees with information, instruction, training and supervision to ensure safety at work.

4 The whole working environment must be free from health and safety risks and the safety of *visitors* (such as customers) is also included.

5 Employers may not charge for anything provided for the employees' safety.

6 Every employer (and the self-employed) must ensure that working activities do not endanger the general public. The government may require that the public is informed of possible threats to their health and safety.

7 Anyone who designs, manufactures, imports or supplies articles for use in the workplace must ensure that they can be used safely and must provide information on how to do this.

8 Work equipment should be suitable for the purpose for which it is used or provided. This includes equipment which has been adapted – it must be suitable for its intended purpose.

Employees have the following duties:

9 Each employee, whilst at work, *must* take reasonable care for the health and safety of self and other persons.

10 Employees must co-operate with the employer to meet the requirements of the legislation; they must report anything which needs repairing or replacing and help to keep the environment free from hazards.

11 No-one must recklessly or intentionally interfere with or misuse anything provided in the interests of health, safety or welfare.

Ensuring customer security

Security procedures in travel mean that people must pass through security checks at airports and there are regulations about what may be carried in the luggage. Money should be kept in a safe place; cheque book and cheque card should be carried separately so that they cannot be stolen and used.

If there are any arguments or verbal abuse from difficult customers, staff should record incidents and try to find out what has caused them. Measures can be decided on to prevent the situation from happening again.

Security of facility and information

A sales outlet can be laid out so that staff can see between display stands and counters. Any blind spots should be watched through mirrors or closed-circuit TV. Stocks may carry tags which can only be moved at the cash point. Expensive items such as watches and jewellery should be stored in a locked cabinet. Windows may have shutters which can be closed at night. Other ways of protecting leisure and tourism places are to have burglar and fire alarms fitted and security guards to patrol the premises.

Information held on computer should only be available to people who have the password. If filing cabinets have private information stored in them, they should be locked. Handbags or cash boxes should be locked away and not left where they can easily be stolen. Private information should never be left on view on a desk or computer screen when the operator leaves the room.

Work in groups of between 2 and 4 people.

Visit a leisure or tourist facility and make notes about the ways in which it is made secure; use your own experience as a user if relevant. There may be notices about what to do in case of fire, rules about ways of dealing with money and goods, safety regulations to protect customers and staff, instructions for handling equipment, suggestions for wearing safety gear or information for customers about risks taken when using equipment or facilities. Notices should point out the fire exits.

You may discuss and exchange information with the rest of your group.

Write an *individual* account of your findings and give the source of your information (list how you or another member of the group found the information).

CORE SKILL: *Communication 1.1 Take part in discussions*
Range 1, 2, 3, 4

Factors affecting customer service

Customer service is affected by whether there are any means of providing it. There must be a sports instructor present before the customer can begin to learn the sport – and the customer must have money to buy the necessary equipment. Leisure centres must have staff who work at all times and not just during the day. If there is no-one to serve in the snack bar, customers go hungry. There must be resources such as computers to give instant answers to questions about the availability of travel or accommodation. Internet (International Network of Computers) links computers which have a modem, telephone line and the correct software. There is a charge for access to the system. There are electronic mail systems using a jotter with a special pen, fax machines which can send and transmit words and pictures. Computer information may also be sent through the telephone network using data links by the British Telecom system called Datel. These resources are very useful to the travel industry and affect the service given to customers.

Other physical resources affecting customer service are facilities and equipment. A water park must have a stretch of water to use; climbing may be practised on an indoor 'climbing wall' but the customer will then wish to use rocks and mountains in a climb.

Finance (money) is another factor affecting customer service.

Large theme parks cost millions of pounds to build and improvements may be made every year, giving better service to the customers when there is money to pay for more rides, facilities and catering.

A leisure facility can vary from a working farm, which has provided picnic benches and play equipment for children in its grounds in order to attract families looking for a day out, to large amenities (such as Center Parcs) which need plenty of finance to set up.

Staff skills and experience are very important when providing customer service. Junior staff learn through training, observing experienced staff and trying to meet the needs of customers.

The initial contact with the customer is important. Greeting the customer politely, trying to find out what the customer needs and then fulfilling his or her expectations is the goal. Staff skills can be enhanced by involving them in discussions about customer care so that they play a part in setting the firm's policy. Training for all staff is important so that they know how to project a caring attitude. Staff should know all about the product or service being provided, be able to talk about it, give the correct price when asked and if an order has to be taken, follow simple procedures laid down. Benefits for the customer should also be described. If there are information leaflets or brochures about the product or service, junior staff should study them in order to know more about it.

Customers who buy a product or service are really buying the expectation that it will give them satisfaction. Sales staff should be able to give information so that customers buy the product they want and need so that the customers find their expectations being met.

The design of the facility will have a bearing on customer service. It may be a privately-run facility, for example a sports fitness centre in a big hotel. It may be a leisure centre owned by the local authority, with swimming pool, hall for indoor football, badminton, keep-fit classes or squash courts. Whatever the complex, it may have a snack bar, cafeteria or restaurants and shops where equipment may be bought. The design will decide what recreational activities can be offered for customers in the facility.

Work with 2 to 3 people.

Select a facility which you can visit, observe or use as a customer.

1 Write down an example of how the facility provides effective customer service and state how this will benefit:

   a the customer, and
   b the facility.

2 The following items can affect the service which is given to the customer:

   ♦ the human resources (people who work there)

   ♦ physical resources (including facilities and equipment used)
   ♦ the financial resources (where the money comes from to run the place)
   ♦ staff skills (qualifications and experience of staff who provide the service)
   ♦ the design of the facility (what does it include?)

Choose two of these items and explain how they benefit the customers who use the facility.

You may use this activity as part of the **Evidence Indicator** for this unit.

Organisations and customer service

Everyone who works in a leisure and tourism organisation can be expected to come into contact with customers. Junior staff are sometimes worried about this – the telephone rings and they look round for someone else to answer it as they are sure they will not know what to say! Observing others, finding out about the organisation and its products and services will all help to give enough confidence to speak to the customer.

Some staff expect to have regular contact with customers. The ticket clerk will explain any procedures to the customer, give directions, explain alternatives and make decisions about whether a child really is as young as the customer is claiming and entitled to a half-price ticket. The sports coach, the general operator on a theme park ride, the hotel receptionist, the security guard and the travel courier will all expect to deal with customers and develop good communication skills.

Other staff have jobs where customer contact may not be expected – the person who is doing the cleaning, the engineer maintaining the rides or the person doing the cooking in the café may not expect to meet customers. However, it is useful for all these staff to have some knowledge and skills of how to

A ticket clerk may also give directions.

deal with customers. They may have to direct people or give them information, such as closing times. They should be prepared to greet customers and answer their questions.

🏃 🏃 🏃 🏃 🏃 **ACTIVITY 5** 🏃 🏃 🏃 🏃 🏃

Work with 2 to 4 people.

1 Discuss in turn any satisfactory or unsatisfactory experiences you may have had with the staff of an organisation providing customer service.

2 Write down a set of rules which you think should be observed by those people who come into contact with customers.

Types of customer service offered

Providing information for the customer is one of the main jobs in providing service. The tourist information centre, your local, school or college library, your local travel agent all have a collection of leaflets on local and regional attractions and the people working there may help customers by suggesting local places of interest to visit. Tourist information centres often have accommodation lists of hotels and guesthouses, and some will book the accommodation for visitors. There may also be books and postcards for sale from the centres or from local shops and stores. Hotel staff or guesthouse owners are often asked for information about places of interest in the locality by visitors.

People working in a leisure facility may be asked to provide information about activities, prices, times and whether classes are full or not. This information could be stored on computer or filed on card index or be available through leaflets and notices.

Besides providing information, staff may be asked to provide advice. Sales staff, sports coaches, hotel receptionists and others who have contact with customers may be asked for their advice and should be prepared for this aspect of their work.

The sports coach may be asked to advise on the best equipment or shoes, the hotel receptionist for the best in local theatres, cinemas, restaurants and shops. Customers must be able to rely on advice provided by staff.

Another aspect of customer service is to provide assistance. Sometimes customers are not at all sure what they really want. The assistant smiles or perhaps greets the customer to see if he or she wants some help. Listen carefully to what the customers say and then repeat it back to them to make sure you have understood it. You can then suggest alternatives for the customers to consider until they decide what they want. If you are asked for your opinion, try to be objective and choose the best for the customer, not the best for you!

Dealing with problems needs tact. If a customer has found the courage to complain to you, the situation must be dealt with immediately. Take a note of his or her name, address and telephone number and then write the complaint down. Listen but do not interrupt. At the end, read back your notes to make sure you have noted everything.

Sympathise with the customer and try to agree on a solution. The Sale of Goods Act (which also covers the sale of a service) says that if a product is faulty, customers are entitled to their money back or an exchange for another one without faults.

If the goods are not faulty, but the customer is simply unhappy about the purchase, some organisations will exchange it or take it back and return the money. This is done so that the unhappy customer is turned into a satisfied one and will come back again.

When the problem has been resolved, make a note in your diary or on your calendar and check up in the near future to see if the result is still satisfactory to the customer.

If the problem is not one with which you can deal yourself, bring in someone with more experience – your supervisor or another assistant with more knowledge than you have.

🏃 🏃 🏃 🏃 🏃 **ACTIVITY 6** 🏃 🏃 🏃 🏃 🏃

Write out the following sentences, filling in the missing word(s).

<u>1</u> A collection of leaflets on local attractions can be found at the _____.

<u>2</u> If customers appear to want assistance, staff should _____ to them carefully.

<u>3</u> Complaints must be dealt with _____.

<u>4</u> If a product is faulty, customers are entitled to _____ _____ _____.

<u>5</u> If you cannot deal with a problem yourself, ask _____ _____.

Product-related customer service

Selling

Many tourist attractions have a souvenir shop next to the exit. The assistants will be responsible for keeping the shop tidy and well stocked, and will know something about the products. For example, goods made by local people may not be available anywhere else and visitors may be attracted to examples of craft work. Other jobs are to price the goods, take stock, communicate with the customers and cash up at the end of the day. There may be shoplifters to deal with: the best way to deter thieves is to have alert and interested shop assistants.

Besides the souvenir shop, there may be a café, restaurant or snack bar. Many of the duties of the staff are similar to those of a shop assistant, although anyone dealing with food may have to have a hygiene certificate.

Coaching

A sports coach works with a group of people, or sometimes with one individual, to teach the basic principles of a sport or to improve skills. People are shown how to use the equipment and the best way of doing things. A coach will have special qualifications in the particular sport, be able to look after the equipment and organise and supervise a group of people. If a coach has more than one specialist sport to offer, there are more opportunities for jobs.

Running outdoor activities

This could be organising matches for various outdoor sports or arranging walking, climbing or rambling activities. Renting out boats or sailboards in a water park or being in charge of tennis courts or golf courses (which can be private or owned by the local authority) is part of this type of job. The organiser will know and operate basic safety procedures, welcome the customers, deal with emergencies and be calm and practical. Knowledge of local weather conditions will also be useful.

Work in groups of 2 to 4 people.

1 Choose a leisure and tourism facility to study (either by observation, work shadowing or using the facility as a customer).

2 Identify an occasion when the organisation provided good customer service. Write a brief account of the occasion and keep it to use as part of your **Evidence indicator** at the end of this element.

Making bookings

This could include a computer system to book theatre or cinema tickets. If a conference is being organised, checking the cost and booking the venue may also be done using a computer. Tourists will also book travel and accommodation through a travel agent using a version of Prestel. Tour operators buy 'space' on this system and develop a private viewdata system which is then accessed by using a password. The travel agent can then use the system to give the customer information about the holidays available.

The booking clerk in any leisure organisation will need good communication skills and be able to handle questions and requests for information, have a good grasp of arithmetic and be able to operate a computer. In some cases cashing up at the end of the shift has to be done. The job may operate during 'unsocial' hours (as in a cinema booking office) so that people can go there in their leisure time.

Serving food and drink

Bar staff, waiters and waitresses and counter assistants in a fast food outlet all need to be able to remember orders, take cash and serve food and drink. Sometimes people who use a restaurant do so to celebrate a special occasion, so the people who serve them can do much to make it a happy occasion.

Shift work (often during the evening and at the weekend) is usual, so staff need to be flexible. They must have basic knowledge of hygiene and may have to operate catering equipment or clean and tidy the place before it opens in preparation for the next session.

Work in the same groups as for Activity 7. Use the same facility (if possible) as you did for Activity 7.

Describe the main types of service provided for customers in the facility you have selected.

You may exchange information but your account must be an individual one. Keep your work to use as part of your **Evidence indicator** at the end of this element. If possible, use a word processor.

Methods of communication with customers

Much of the information which is given to customers is face-to-face or over the telephone. It is important to remember to use simple language when you are giving information. Speak clearly and more slowly than you would normally do. Practise at home in front of a mirror to see how it looks to others when you give information. If you want a stern critic, a small brother, sister, niece or nephew will be completely honest about whether he or she can hear and understand you! Alternatively, you may wish to practise by having a video made and then watch it, looking for ways in which you might improve.

Watching someone who is more expert than you is useful – you may pick up some useful tips. People giving information to customers are all around us so it should not be too difficult to find some examples.

Giving information to customers

Individual customers

When a person approaches someone working in a leisure and tourism firm for information, that person may not be free because he or she is speaking to another customer or is using the telephone. The new customer should be greeted with a smile, to acknowledge his or her presence, and attended to as quickly as soon as possible.

Greet customers with 'Good morning' or 'Good afternoon' as appropriate. Some organisations teach their staff to say 'How may I help you?' The word 'may' is used instead of 'can', because 'may' means to allow whilst 'can' means to be able to. 'Can I help you?' could provoke the reply, 'I don't know, *can* you?' by someone who insists on accurate English. Helpfulness and courtesy are essential when giving information. If you do not know the answer, ask a more experienced member of staff or say you will find out and let the customer know. Always follow this up; customers are valuable and an enquiry may very well turn into a booking and a satisfied customer.

Groups of customers

Staff who give information to groups may be representatives for a tour operator or guides showing people round a facility. Whatever the occasion it is important to speak up clearly and allow time for questions from the audience. Usually tour guides have a signal to let groups know that they wish to speak, for example they may hold a hand up in the air for silence. Tour representatives usually follow up their information with a leaflet to remind groups of what they have said. Again, speak more clearly and slowly than you would normally do if you want to be sure that the group has heard you and repeat important points in case someone was not listening the first time. Be patient with anyone who asks a question which you have already answered – not everyone has perfect hearing.

ACTIVITY 9

The city of Chester was known as Deva in Roman times and tourists are surprised to see Roman soldiers, dressed in full regalia, reporting for duty at the East Gate early in the morning to conduct tourists on a guided tour of the city. This original way of showing people

the historical sites attracts tourists who enjoy being shown what history was like as well as hearing about it.

The guides have to do some serious historical research in order to introduce the tourists to the well-preserved Roman sites and people can see for themselves the body armour, helmets, shields and swords which were once carried by Roman soldiers.

Guides have to keep a balance between educating visitors and entertaining them. The Roman Empire was built on a system of slavery and the guides try to show tourists both sides of life.

Answer the following questions in full sentences.

1 What is the advantage of having 'Roman soldiers' as tourist guides in Chester?

2 How do the guides obtain their information?

3 What balance do tourist guides have to keep?

4 From your knowledge of giving information to groups, write a short account of how the Roman soldier tourist guides might give information to the groups of people they are taking round the city.

Customers of different ages

Anyone who has had to give information to children will realise that it has to be repeated (sometimes more than once) to hit that peak in their attention span when they are actually listening. Use simple language and check that they do know what you have just said by asking questions.

People tend to switch off when they are told something which they do not want to know, so this has to be sandwiched between information in which they are interested. Use terms which your customers understand.

Older people may be hard of hearing so information which is followed up by a leaflet might be useful. Face people when you talk to them, move your lips properly and use gestures and facial expressions.

Customers from different cultural backgrounds

People from different cultural backgrounds may have ideas and attitudes which differ very much from those in the UK and it is important to remember this when giving information.

Body language is different in other cultural backgrounds. People born in the UK may be used to looking the person they are addressing straight in the eye, whereas in some cultures this is considered rude. People from other cultures may have rules about what women should wear; they may be required to cover arms and legs.

When visitors from the UK go abroad, they may find that the cultural background in the country they visit bans alcohol or does not allow women to drive. When visiting churches or cathedrals abroad, people may cause offence if they arrive in holiday shorts and vests and may be asked to wear something over them. Women may be required to wear something over their heads.

One of your jobs in the holiday industry, whether at home or abroad, may be to advise people of the requirements of different cultural backgrounds and to know about and allow for any differences when you give information.

Some cultures do not eat certain foods, or they may only eat meat which has been killed in a certain way. If catering is involved, you may have to give information about the food and the way it is prepared. Often, vegetarian meals will meet cultural requirements.

Information should be carefully prepared and given to customers in a way which does not give offence, and checks should be made once you have given the information to make sure it has been properly understood.

Non-English speaking customers

Many people working in the leisure and tourist industry are able to speak another language so that they can converse with non-English speaking customers. If the language of your customer is one which you do not know, a collection of phrase-books where customers can find the question in their own language and point it out to you is useful. Written information in the customers' own language that you can hand to them is also helpful. Pen and paper for pictures and diagrams also play their part, as does body language. You may point something out, or use facial expressions and gestures. The universal sign for 'Yes' is to nod the head, and shaking it from side to side means 'no'.

Customer service by going the extra step to show your client how to get somewhere or where facilities are, is essential in this context.

Customers with specific needs

When you give information to people with specific needs, make sure you do so with sensitivity. Wheelchair users can answer you – do not speak only to the person who is with them. If you are speaking to hearing-impaired people, you may need to draw their attention by gently touching their arm. Face them when you speak and move your lips slowly and clearly as they may be able to lip-read what you say.

Make sure there are no obstacles in the way of sight-impaired people and tell them about any notices or other information which they cannot read.

People who have difficulty with reading and writing may make excuses and ask you to fill in forms for them by saying that they have 'forgotten their glasses' so be tactful and helpful. You may have to give them information verbally and ask questions to make sure that they have understood it. This may also apply to people who have difficulty with numbers.

Work with a partner or in a small group.

_1_ Choose a facility that you know as a customer, or from work shadowing or work experience.

_2_ Walk round the facility, observe and write down all the _signs_ which would communicate with all the customers in the categories you have just been reading about. For example, a sign showing a fire extinguisher might look like this:

You may find other examples to show fire exits, to identify toilet facilities, to forbid smoking.

_3_ Draw these signs neatly and label them.

Types of customer communication

Face-to-face communication

Staff in leisure and tourism facilities meet many of their customers in face-to-face situations and need to develop the communication skills of listening and speaking. Greeting people with a smile gives a pleasant first impression. A regional accent is not as important as speaking clearly and pronouncing words properly with the endings in place. Think before you speak and use pauses to allow the listener to follow what you are saying. At the end, check that you have been understood. Do not use dialect words or slang.

Listen carefully when a customer speaks to you. You may wish to take notes, particularly if a customer is complaining. Read the notes back to make sure that all the points have been recorded. If you do not write notes, say the points back to the customer to show that you have been listening.

Written communication

This could be memos, letters, advertising leaflets, notices and press releases. You may have to write to people above or below you in your organisation, to individual customers, to groups or to the general public. It is important to think of the tone when using written communication and to be formal rather than casual. In all organisations, it is important for co-operation that everyone knows what is happening. Some firms have regular newsletters or magazines giving information to staff.

Letters and memos usually have a paragraph which introduces the topic, a middle paragraph which expands it and a final paragraph or sentence which tells the reader what the writer now expects to happen. For example, a memo informing staff about a new product or service which is going to be offered may finish by stating how they can get to know about it.

Advantages of written communication are that the receiver can study it to make sure the contents have been understood. The writer also keeps a copy of the message. Disadvantages are that written communications take longer to compose, to travel to their destination and are quite expensive because of the time needed to write and then word process them.

Telephone communication

Within a very short space of time, staff using the telephone can be in touch with people all over the world. Information can be provided, questions answered, products sold and orders received and placed. Services can be improved and a good impression made on customers by using a friendly, helpful and polite telephone manner.

If you have to make a call, have the number and all the information you are going to need ready before you begin. You may need to make notes, so keep a pen and paper handy. Use the hand you do not write with to hold the telephone. Allow enough time for the person at the other end to answer (at least eight or nine rings). First of all give your name and that of your organisation. State who you wish to talk to and, if the call is going to be lengthy, ask if the person has time to talk.

When you answer the telephone, have your pen and paper ready to make notes. Try to answer promptly and identify yourself and/or your department. Be friendly and polite. If the call is for someone else who is not present, ask:

1 if the caller wants to hold whilst you find the person

2 if you can take a message

3 if the caller wants the call to be returned

4 if the caller wants to call again.

In the last case, try to give an indication of when someone will be available to receive the call.

Do not use technical terms unless the caller is likely to understand them. Speak clearly and more slowly than you would do in a face-to-face situation. Listen carefully and then re-state what the caller has said in your own words and do not let anyone else in the room distract or interrupt you. If you are the person for whom a telephone message is taken, deal with it promptly and ring back as soon as possible.

Advantages of using the telephone are that there is usually an instant reply, questions can be answered or information given immediately and a friendly but business-like relationship with the customer can be established. It is often cheaper than writing.

Disadvantages are that there is no record of a telephone conversation and details may have to be confirmed in writing. Other countries may be difficult to contact during the hours you are at work because of the time difference. Long-distance telephone calls can be expensive.

ACTIVITY 11

Work with a partner.

Imagine a new member of staff is using the following expressions when speaking to customers on the telephone. Decide on a more appropriate expression for each one and write it down. Check with your tutor.

1 'Hang on!'

2 'He's out.'

3 'What?'

4 'There's no-one here who can tell you.'

5 'Wait a minute.'

How to do a report

The first thing to remember about a report is that it is **impersonal** so you cannot use 'I found out . . . I visited . . . I looked up . . .' Instead you should write: 'It was found . . . a visit was made . . . books were consulted'.

The next thing is to recognise that formal reports have several parts to them. These are usually:

▶ **terms of reference**
▶ **procedure** (sometimes called **method**)
▶ **findings**
▶ **conclusion(s)**
▶ **recommendation(s)**.

The **terms of reference** contain the heading of the report and what it is all about.

The **procedure** or **method** states how the information for the report was obtained. 'It was observed that . . .' would be the way the person writing the report shows that the information was gathered by watching someone or something.

Findings is all the information put together logically. Sometimes this is done in numbered paragraphs if there is a lot of information.

Conclusion(s) is where you state what you decide about the subject at the end of the report.

Recommendation(s) may be left out if this is not appropriate; otherwise it is where the person writing the report makes suggestions about what ought to be done.

Evidence indicator

A brief report is required, giving examples from your investigation of customer service needs in one leisure and tourism facility. You may use the facility you have already investigated for your activities, but you will need to go back and obtain more evidence for the report.

1 State in general terms the benefits of providing effective customer service.

2 Give an example of this from:

   a meeting customers' needs
   b ensuring health and safety (this could be of the customers, the facility, your colleagues or yourself)
   c ensuring security (this could be of the customers, the facility, of information, your colleagues or yourself).

3 State how the selected facility can benefit from effective customer service.

4 Look at the factors affecting customer service, such as:

   a the availability of resources (human, physical and financial)
   b staff skills
   c customers' expectations
   d the design of the facility.

   Give three examples from these factors which apply to the facility you have chosen and say how they affect service to customers.

5 Look at the occasions when your selected facility provides customer service and choose five examples of this. Three of the examples must be when contact with the customer is expected (when it is part of someone's main job) and

two examples of unexpected customer contact (when someone such as a maintenance person or cleaner has contact which is not really part of his or her main job).

Write down the five examples you have chosen. Give examples of the methods of communication used in these examples.

6 What are the main types of service provided for customers in the facility you have chosen? Choose from:

- providing information
- providing advice
- providing assistance
- dealing with problems
- providing product-related services (such as selling, coaching, running outdoor activities, making bookings, serving food and drinks).

Give examples of the methods of communication with customers which are used when offering service (such as face-to-face, telephone and written communication).

When you have gathered your information, write up your report *individually* starting with the terms of reference below.

A report on an investigation into the customer service needs of . . . . (*complete the line with the organisation of your choice*)

If possible, use a word processor.

Evaluation

Once you have completed the work for this unit, you are asked to evaluate it. This means to judge what you have done against the original activity you were asked to do.

1 First, check that you have done everything.

2 Does your work cover all the things you were asked to do?

3 What were the advantages of the method you used?

4 What were the disadvantages of other methods which you decided not to use?

5 Can you state how the work might have been improved?

Write out a short statement about this and head it 'Evaluation'.

Revision and specimen test questions

Each of the multiple choice questions which follow shows more than one possible answer: *a*, *b*, *c* or *d*, but only *one* is correct. Decide which answer is correct and write it down in your notebook.

The correct answers are given at the end of the book so that you can check your responses.

Focus 1: Customer service

Reference: Element 1.1 PC1, PC2, PC3

External test requirements

a *Recognise the benefits of providing effective customer service and identify examples for given facilities.*

Range

Benefits

When an organisation provides effective customer service, the benefits are that there will be **increased sales**. The business will have an **enhanced reputation** as customers speak well of it to other people. Satisfied customers will come back and this will lead to **repeat business**.

1 A benefit to a travel agency of providing effective customer service would be that customers would:
   a only want to travel abroad
   b feel that they were a nuisance to the staff
   c book their holidays with the same firm year after year
   d use Teletext to book their own holidays

2 A leisure centre has staff who are very helpful to both long standing and new customers. This will lead to the customers:
   a using the centre only if they have their own transport
   b wearing the latest formal fashions
   c wanting to be spectators all the time
   d telling other people how good the centre is

3 A souvenir shop in a theme park has staff who take the trouble to show gifts which are not too dear to parties of school children who cannot afford the expensive things on offer. This will lead to:
   a a loss of profit
   b increased sales
   c disappointment for the children
   d complaints from the teachers

Range

Benefits

There are benefits to yourself as a member of staff when you provide effective customer service. You will have increased satisfaction in your job, which in turn could lead to better job prospects and promotion.

4 A benefit of providing effective customer service to a sports coach in a leisure centre is:
   a he or she will feel more satisfaction with the work
   b he or she will become impatient with people who do not listen

c customers will want information about a rival leisure centre

d customers will expect to pay extra for the coaching

5 A fast food counter assistant would benefit from providing effective customer service by:

a leaving all the work to a trainee

b never speaking to the people being served

c being friendly and cheerful towards the customers

d looking forward to the end of the shift

Range

Benefits

The customer is buying the expectation of being satisfied. The benefits to the customer of effective customer service are increased satisfaction and a safe and secure environment.

6 A librarian in the local authority library made it a habit to smile at nervous-looking students. One student was wondering whether she could ask where to find a book on customer service. When she saw the smile, she felt that:

a the librarian saw her as a nuisance

b the librarian was signalling that she would help

c the librarian was laughing at her

d the librarian was not interested in her

7 The riding school instructor asked the young rider to try on a riding hat for size before mounting a pony. This was an example of:

a making the rider feel silly

b instructing the person in riding technique

c looking for an excuse to refuse to instruct the rider

d providing a safe environment

Range

Effective customer service

For customer service to be effective, it should meet the needs of customers and ensure their health and safety as well as that of self, colleagues and the facility.

8 Customers' needs are most likely to be met if:

a they are allowed to look round without being pressured to buy

b there is no information available about products

c the assistant urges them to buy

d they have no idea what they want and leave quickly

Range

Effective customer service

It is important to ensure health and safety when people are taking part in sporting activities. They may need special safety gear to be worn (such as hats, helmets, safety harness, life-jackets, boots and special clothing). Information on how to use the equipment must also be provided.

9 Which two of the following are health and safety needs of customers?

1 riding hats to be worn when pony trekking

2 life-jackets to be used when canoeing

3 supervision by staff who are training for a qualification

4 inflatables should be put in the water when swimming

Choose from:

a 1 and 2

b 2 and 3

c 3 and 4

d 1 and 4

To ensure safety of customers, staff and colleagues it is necessary to keep the place in which you work free from hazards and dangers. Wet floors must have notices so that people do not slip, fire exits should be marked with notices giving directions, all emergency exits should be left clear. Any supervision should be given only by trained staff. Employees must take care of themselves and other people. Activities undertaken must not endanger the general public. Things which need repairing must be reported and mended as soon as possible.

10 To ensure the health and safety of self, leisure and tourism staff should:
   a give customers information about safety product prices
   b make sure that the working environment is clean and tidy
   c stress the health-giving benefits of sports to children
   d help the customer to make informed choices of snacks

11 Ensuring the health and safety of colleagues would be helped by:
   a putting away any 'what to do in case of fire' notices
   b giving an untrained sports coach a class to take
   c keeping emergency exits clear at all times
   d checking the organisation's policy on complaints

The facility is kept safe by making sure there are no dangers. For example, in a theme park the machinery and equipment must be checked regularly and records kept. Anything which has been adapted must be suitable for the intended purpose.

12 To make sure that the facility is safe, technicians in a leisure park would:
   a have 'at your own risk' printed on tickets
   b refuse to let any children on the rides

   c service machinery and equipment regularly
   d count how many adults use the facilities

Range

Effective customer service

Security of customers, colleagues and of self means that people must accept security checks when travelling by air.

Keeping money in a safe place helps customer security.

Self and colleagues should record incidents when their own security has been threatened by abuse from customers and measures should be taken to prevent the situation from happening again.

13 The ticket issuing clerk for rides in a theme park needed to leave the booth for a few minutes. Which two of the following security measures should be taken?
   1 ask a customer to look after the booth
   2 lock the till
   3 lock the booth
   4 ask a security guard to check when he has time

   Choose from:
   a 1 and 2
   b 2 and 3
   c 3 and 4
   d 1 and 4

14 The security staff at the airport ask a customer to step on one side and be searched. The customer refuses. This means that:
   a the security staff will try persuasion
   b the customer may refuse but cannot then board the aircraft
   c the security staff let the customer go without searching

d the customer will complain and get a refund

A sales facility can be made more secure if staff can see display stands and counters. Mirrors and closed-circuit TV can be used. Expensive items should be locked up. Burglar and fire alarms may be fitted; security guards may be used.

15 A snack bar assistant found that chocolate bars on top of the counter were being taken and not paid for. Which of the following methods would be most likely to solve this problem?
   a she decides never to turn her back to the counter
   b she puts the chocolate bars in a box on the counter
   c she watches the waiting customers carefully when serving others
   d she puts the chocolate bars under the counter

Information held on computer should be available only to those who have the password. Work should not be left on screen when the operator has left the room. Filing cabinets with confidential information should be locked; cash boxes and handbags locked in a desk drawer.

16 A hotel receptionist asked a guest for her credit card number and then repeated it in front of other people. This was an instance of:
   a ensuring security
   b using a computer information password
   c giving out secret information
   d ignoring the needs of the other guests

External test requirements

b *Recognise the factors which affect customer service, and identify examples for given facilities.*

Range

Availability of resources

Resources are the means of supplying what is required and can be people, objects or money. This can also include the skills of the staff, the equipment and the natural environment.

17 Customer service given by a travel agent can be affected by:
   a the popularity of a customer
   b the room service in any hotel
   c the local authority leisure complex
   d up-to-date computer systems with information on travel

18 A sports centre advertises for a trampolining coach but does not receive replies from suitable candidates. This means that the customers:
   a are supervised by the swimming coach
   b cannot use the trampoline
   c can practise by themselves without any supervision
   d will be offered a computer course instead

Range

Customers' expectations

Customers who pay for a service are really buying the hope that it will give them satisfaction. The facility which they use will be an important part of this – besides recreational facilities, they will want a snack bar, toilet facilities and perhaps somewhere to buy the equipment.

19 Customers would expect a local authority swimming pool to have:
   a a swimming coach always available to give lessons
   b a licensed bar near to the pool side
   c staff with life-saving qualifications on duty
   d a shop selling swimwear

External test requirements

c *Recognise occasions when organisations provide customer service, and identify examples for given facilities.*

All workers in leisure and tourism may expect to come into contact with customers – to provide information, directions, help, advice and instructions.

20 Which two of the following would an assistant in a tourist information centre in a seaside town expect to provide to customers?
  1 information about holidays in America
  2 an estimate of the number of foreign visitors in town
  3 accommodation lists of local hotels and guesthouses
  4 leaflets about local places to visit

  Choose from:
  a 1 and 2
  b 2 and 3
  c 3 and 4
  d 1 and 4

21 A climbing coach demonstrates the use of a safety harness and shows the group how to wear it. This is an example of giving customers:
  a instructions
  b sport
  c equipment
  d regulations

Focus 2: Providing service for customers

Reference: Element 1.1 PC4, PC5

External test requirements

a *Recognise the main types of service provided for customers in given facilities.*

Range

Main types of service

Customers look to the staff for information, advice, assistance, help in dealing with problems and they look for a product-related service (such as a souvenir shop near the exit of a zoo to provide them with a memento of their visit). They may also expect to see snack bars, cafés, ice-cream booths, programmes, maps and information leaflets. If they have a particular problem (such as a member of the group who is a wheelchair user) then they may need help in solving any problems.

22 To be able to give information, the assistant in a tourist information centre should know:
  a where to find the information in the centre
  b who runs the local football team
  c every leisure and recreation place in the area
  d who is on the duty rota in the kitchens at a local hotel

23 Customers need advice from a travel agent on:
  a whether the agent prefers the Channel Tunnel or the ferry to cross the sea
  b where to find telesales holidays
  c whether the customer's outfit is tasteful
  d whether a holiday resort is suitable for teenagers

24 Which two of the following activities are part of the job of baggage handling staff who have had training in dealing with customers at an airport?
  1 writing out customs forms
  2 taking wheelchair users out to the plane

3 telling travellers which check-in desk to use

4 cleaning the kitchens for the airport café

Choose from:

a 1 and 2

b 2 and 3

c 3 and 4

d 1 and 4

When a product or service is offered, there are other related services which are needed. Selling, coaching and running outdoor activities are part of the leisure scene.

25 Customers of a leisure centre who are part of the football team need:

a information about crowd numbers

b somewhere to buy their strip

c assistance with getting ready for the match

d regular weeks with no training

26 Which two of the following would someone running an outdoor activity be expected to do as part of the job?

1 booking a sports field for a fixture

2 arranging for a swimming gala at an indoor pool

3 advertising for a sports centre manager

4 checking necessary staff are available for a match

Choose from:

a 1 and 2

b 2 and 3

c 3 and 4

d 1 and 4

Making bookings is an important part of all leisure and tourism or recreation services. Travel, accommodation, catering and sports facilities all need advance booking so that they can be used to their fullest extent.

Food and drink can be served in places ranging from an expensive restaurant to a snack bar by the local swimming pool. All places which serve food and drink must keep health and safety laws.

27 A receptionist in a leisure centre would make bookings for the main hall using:

a an account book

b a current bookings sheet

c a notepad by the telephone

d any handy piece of paper

28 Which two of the following would a fast food organisation expect its counter hands to do?

1 get all the food out of the refrigerator when the shift begins

2 wear their own clothes when serving the food and drink

3 wash their hands frequently as requested by the employer

4 clean the work surfaces regularly

Choose from:

a 1 and 2

b 2 and 3

c 3 and 4

d 1 and 4

External test requirements

b *Identify examples of different methods of communication with customers in given facilities.*

Range

Methods of communication: face-to-face, telephone, written

Communication can be face-to-face speaking either to groups or individuals. It can be written by hand, typed, word processed or the telephone can be used. Speak slowly and clearly face-to-face and when telephoning. Draft your written communications and then check through them. Use the spell-check on the computer for greater accuracy and follow the conventions for writing letters, memos and reports.

29 Which method of communication would be most suitable for a tour guide to use with a group of people?
   a hand signals and body language only
   b give out leaflets with pictures only
   c ensure everyone has a walkman with recorded information
   d speak slowly and clearly, face-to-face

30 A customer who is at work all day wishes to reserve seats for the next evening's performance at a theatre in a nearby town. The most likely way to book the seats would be to:
   a telephone and use a credit card to pay over the telephone
   b go to the theatre and buy the tickets with cash
   c send a letter first-class with a cheque
   d wait at the theatre next evening hoping for returned tickets

31 A hotel manager speaks to a young couple and their parents about the arrangements for their wedding. When all the decisions have been made, the manager would most likely confirm them by:
   a a telephone call to say it would be all right
   b a visit from the manager to the bride's parents
   c a letter confirming all the arrangements and receipt of deposit
   d a postcard from the manager to say arrangements were proceeding

element 1.2

Provide service to leisure and tourism customers

In this element, given customer situations are role-played by students so that they can try to meet the service needs of customers. This is achieved when customers are satisfied. Students should also deliver the 'extra element' in customer care which costs nothing to either the firm or the member of staff – a positive attitude.

The simulations which make up a greater part of the activities give situations which might arise in a variety of leisure and recreational contexts. Besides playing the members of staff giving a service, students are also called upon to *be* the customers for their colleagues. If students are also able to obtain experience in work situations, these may also be used to complement the simulated experiences suggested here.

Before beginning the activities, students should read through this chapter and map out a plan of action giving the order in which the activities will take place and the projected dates and times. If alterations have to be made to the plan, they must be recorded. This plan is the working document which shows the student what is being achieved.

ACTIVITY 1

Work in two groups, A and B.

1 Decide on a possible organisation for which your particular group works. Then decide on the standards which you will try to apply to your work with customers. For example, you may decide to answer the telephone before the *fourth* ring. Work out how you will:

▶ satisfy customer needs
▶ exceed customer needs
▶ project a caring attitude towards customers

▶ show a positive attitude to your work.

Each group writes down the standards which they hope to achieve in customer care and every member of the group writes or word processes an individual copy to keep.

2 At the end of each simulation, check back with your standards to see if you have achieved them. When you evaluate your work, refer back to this.

Providing effective
customer service

It is important for all staff in a leisure or tourism job to gain knowledge about the product or service as quickly as possible. There will probably be a training period for new staff to enable them to give information and advice to customers. This may include:

- giving information about the cost
- mentioning any special features
- suggesting suitable alternatives
- help with problems
- pointing out incentives (i.e. free travel insurance)
- handing out leaflets, brochures, or pointing out notices.

Staff should expect to provide assistance if necessary. This could include:

- arranging special facilities for disabled people
- filling in forms for customers (who may not be able to read or write well)
- escorting customers
- assisting customers with enquiries
- following up customer complaints.

It is important for staff to keep calm when working under pressure. They may have to solve problems using the telephone, computer or fax or by suggesting where customers can obtain car hire, exchange their money or even find them another aeroplane if they are called home urgently or have missed their flight.

Since any leisure or tourism operation runs on teamwork there are many staff who support the 'front desk' so it is important to get on well with colleagues and to appreciate the contribution they make to the smooth working of the facility.

Besides the product or service being offered, the facility also has staff who sell it. The travel agent who knows which customer likes a quiet resort and which one is interested in a lively holiday is giving good service in a sales situation. The sports coach who remembers the names of the class members is treating the customers as individuals and making them feel important.

Staff may run outdoor activities. This may include:

- planning a list of fixtures
- choosing the teams and substitutes
- informing the players of dates, times and places of practices and matches
- checking that the necessary staff are available
- booking fields, courts or sports halls
- arranging the necessary transport
- checking equipment and any special clothing.

Most leisure and recreational facilities have somewhere which serves food and drink. Food preparation areas are subject to health and safety laws and staff must ensure that rules given to them by employers are kept. These may include:

- washing hands every half hour
- keeping cooked and uncooked food separately
- throwing away any food brought out of the refrigerator but not eaten that day
- putting all rubbish immediately into closed containers
- keeping all work surfaces clean
- making sure all equipment is clean
- using separate refrigerators for cooked and uncooked meats
- cleaning the floor regularly
- keeping all food in containers or boxes.

ACTIVITY 2

Write out the following sentences, filling in the missing word(s).

1 It is important for all leisure and tourism staff to gain knowledge about the _____ or _____ as quickly as possible.

2 Trained staff will be able to give customers information about the _____ of a product or service.

3 If a customer's first choice is not available, staff should _____ some suitable alternatives.

4 Providing assistance to customers may include _____ special facilities for disabled people.

5 Customers may need assistance when they are making _____.

6 When solving problems, it is important for staff to keep _____.

7 Leisure and tourism operations run on _____ and many people make a contribution to the smooth working of the facility.

8 An example of good sales staff is the sports coach who _____ the names of the individuals in the class.

9 When running outdoor activities, one job is to inform the _____ of the dates, times and places of matches.

10 Food preparation staff must make sure that _____ and _____ rules given to them by the employer are kept.

The customer's buying decisions are influenced by the customer service received. Leisure and tourism staff should keep the needs of their customers in mind when they are doing their work. Being helpful, ensuring everyone's health and safety; keeping customers, the facility and any information secure does not cost any more than doing the work in a sloppy manner. It is important to keep customer needs in mind; without customers there would be no need for the services and products offered and in the end, no need for jobs in leisure and tourism. See Unit 1 to review customer service details.

When you speak to groups of people, you must obtain their attention and interest so that they are ready to listen to you. When you have given your information, check that it has been understood.

ACTIVITY 3

Split into groups of 8 to 10 people and number each person in the group from 1 to 10. Assume that people in the group have come to stay at your school or college for a two-day conference. Each person in the group is going to give information to the rest of the group *clearly*. Catch the attention of the group before beginning to speak. Begin with person 1. Tell the group the following information:

- person 1: where the group is going to eat
- person 2: where the library is situated
- person 3: where to find the hall (or room used as the conference room)
- person 4: what the signal for a fire alarm is, and what procedures the group should follow
- person 5: how to find the toilets and the lifts
- person 6: where the car park is and any restrictions on its use
- person 7: who are the first-aiders and how to contact them
- person 8: where the nearest public telephone is situated
- person 9: how to find the nearest chemist
- person 10: how to find the nearest Post Office.

If the group is small, people may need to be given more than one piece of information.

Word process a short account of how you gave your information. Decide whether you could improve on your performance and say how you would do this (for example, did you speak loudly enough?)

Work in pairs. One of you (Partner A) is a hotel receptionist and the other (Partner B) is a guest. Choose two situations each from the following.

Situation A – need for information

The guest arrives at reception to pay the bill and wishes to book accommodation for next week but the receptionist states that the hotel is full. He or she then gives the guest the names, addresses and telephone numbers of two other local hotels which might have vacancies. (Information for this can be obtained from *Yellow Pages*.)

Situation B – need for advice

The guest comes to reception and asks where the local theatre is situated. The receptionist advises the guest that it would be best to go by taxi and suggests two or three theatres or cinemas, offering advice on the best choice after finding out the guest's tastes.

Situation C – need for assistance

The guest arrives at reception and says that the shower in his or her room is not working properly. The receptionist obtains details and assures the guest that someone will be along to repair it as soon as possible.

Situation D – making a booking

For this situation, the guest telephones the receptionist. If possible use an internal telephone in a different room so that communication is more effective. Remember to have a pen and paper handy to take details down. At the end of the telephone call, the receptionist should read all the details back to the guest, who confirms them.

The guest telephones and explains that he or she wishes to book the hotel's conference room for the last weekend in April (take the correct date from a calendar) from Saturday morning at 0900 hours until Sunday evening at 1800 hours. The name of the company is Mosstown Products Ltd. Accommodation is also required for 22 delegates, four of whom will require single rooms and the others require twin-bedded rooms, all with en-suite facilities.

Write down details of the booking; read back to the guest to check.

Situation E – running outdoor activities

Work individually in this situation.

Your sports tutor has asked you to make arrangements for a fixture (you may choose the sport yourself) for a school or college team to take place on a Wednesday afternoon in two weeks' time.

Make a plan of all the things you would need to do and put them in order of priority (for example, you will need to book the venue first or there will be no point in contacting the team!)

When you are happy with your role-play, ask your tutor to observe you.

Meeting customers' needs

Written communication

Communication which is written, typed or word processed can be sent by letter or by **fax** (which stands for Facsimile Transfer). The equipment used, which is known as a **transceiver**, can transmit and receive all kinds of messages including written materials and pictures. Messages can be sent over the public telephone networks, private lines or by satellite. The fax number of the receiver is dialled like a telephone number and the information placed in the transceiver. When it has been sent, a print-out stating the time and date of the transmission gives proof to the sender. It is received almost at once by the organisation to which it has been sent. A written reply can be faxed back immediately.

Business letters use letter headings which have printed details of the organisation's name and address, the telephone and fax numbers and sometimes a logo.

ACTIVITY 5

Work in pairs. Compose a fax for the following situations.

Partner A
You work in a travel agency and have arranged a ferry booking for a group of college students on the ferry from Ramsgate to Dunkirk on 17 May (this year). The party wish to stay at the Dunkirk Youth Hostel for the evening of 17 May but you have just received a letter to say that they cannot accommodate the party. However, you have booked the group in at Des Fontaines Youth Hostel in Brugge on 18 May. Write a fax to Des Fontaines (whose warden understands English) asking if the group may stay on both 17 and 18 May. Ask for an urgent reply.

Partner B
You work in a travel agency and have arranged a ferry booking for a group of college students to return on the ferry from Dunkirk to Ramsgate on 19 May (this year). However, they have decided to stay in Brussels for an extra day and now wish to embark from Ostend on 20 May. Send a fax to South Sea Ferries, Wharf Office, Ramsgate, asking if it is possible to change the booking so that the party can leave from Ostend instead of Dunkirk on 20 and not 19 May and ask them to confirm in writing as quickly as possible.

You work for a Heritage Working Museum and receive the following letter.

SUNNINGDALE HIGH SCHOOL
Castlefield Road
Greengate
HALTON   Y3 8FL

Head teacher: J. McDonald BA

Tel: 0171 489 2986
Fax: 0171 489 2987

16 September (this year)

The Heritage Working Museum
8 Main Street
GLOUCESTER
GL9 7ER

Dear Sirs

I would like to arrange a visit to the Museum for a class of 28 pupils from Year 11. We would like to experience the sights, sounds and smells of the original textile processes undertaken by a woollen mill as advertised by you in your leaflet as this would be helpful to a history project.

We would like to have a tour with a guide any Wednesday in November from approximately 1000 hours until 1230 hours, leaving about 1330 hours after lunch. Is it possible for the pupils to obtain sandwiches and drinks to eat on the premises?

If you can accommodate the group, please let me know as soon as possible.

Yours faithfully

A. Bailey

A. Bailey
Head of Humanities Department

Design a letter heading for The Heritage Working Museum on a computer. Add a telephone and a fax number to the address.

CORE SKILL: *Information Technology 1.2 Process information*
PC 1, 2, 3, 4, 5
Range 1, 2, 3, 4, 5

Composing a business letter

When you are writing a business letter, think of the reader. Ask yourself: 'What does the reader need to know?' Use this checklist for your letters:

▶ is it plain?
▶ is it short?
▶ is it polite?
▶ is it free from errors?

Your letters must be easy to follow. Do not use long words or sentences.

Beginnings and endings

The following salutations (beginnings) go with the complimentary closes (the endings) shown here:

Dear Sir (or Dear Sirs, or Dear Madam)   Yours faithfully
Dear Mr Jones (or Mrs Brown)   Yours sincerely
Dear Ryan (or Nicola)   Yours sincerely

Remember that if you put 'since' and 'rely' together, they spell 'sincerely'.

If you have met a person, or if you address a person by name, the ending is 'Yours sincerely', otherwise use 'Yours faithfully'.

Middles

In the first paragraph, say what the letter is about. If you are writing on behalf of the firm always use 'we'. This is because you are writing on behalf of the firm, which has many people working for it. 'We have received your letter . . .' is correct, not 'I have received your letter . . .'

In the second paragraph, give any more information which is needed by the reader.

In the last paragraph, say what you want the reader to do about your letter. You may wish to end with:

'We hope to hear from you as soon as possible.'

'We look forward to the goods being delivered by next Wednesday.'

If you do not want the reader to do anything else, you could say:

'If you need any more help or information, please let us know.'

Readers then know that, unless they need more help or information, they need do nothing more.

🏃 🏃 🏃 🏃 🏃 **ACTIVITY 7** 🏃 🏃 🏃 🏃 🏃

Using the letter heading for The Heritage Working Museum in Activity 6 that you have designed, write a reply to the letter from Sunningdale High School. Choose a suitable Wednesday and suggest it for the visit. Confirm that you have booked a tour guide and state that there is a café on the premises where the pupils may obtain a hot drink and buy sandwiches.

Sign the letter with your own name and your position, which is Customer Liaison Clerk.

CORE SKILL: *Communication 1.2 Produce written material*
Range 1, 2, 3 (Format: outline), 4

🏃 🏃 🏃 🏃 🏃 **ACTIVITY 8** 🏃 🏃 🏃 🏃 🏃

Write out the following sentences, filling in the missing word(s).

1 It is important for staff to keep _____ when working under pressure.

2 When you have given information to a group of people, _____ to make sure that it has been understood.

3 When you make a telephone call, remember to have paper and _____ handy.

4 A fax machine can transmit written materials and _____.

5 When writing letters, the beginning 'Dear Sirs' goes with the ending _____ _____.

6 If you have met the person to whom you are writing, or if you begin the letter with his or her name, the ending is 'Yours _____'.

7 In the last paragraph of the letter, state what you want the _____ to do about the letter.

8 If you are writing a letter on behalf of the firm, you should use '_____' and not 'I'.

Prompt service

Case study

Mrs Ashworth decided that she would like to buy some new make-up. As she liked the idea of make-up which had not been tested on animals, she always used Booths' own brand.

Once in the shop, it wasn't difficult to choose from the range on display at the make-up counter. Mrs Ashworth nearly always bought a repeat of the same products which she decided some time ago were just what she wanted. Once she had made her choice, Mrs Ashworth waited patiently for the assistant to notice her and attend to her. However, the assistant seemed to be busily talking to another girl and they both ignored the customer.

'Ahem!' said Mrs Ashworth. This brought a sour look from the assistant doing all the talking. Mrs Ashworth sighed. She waited. The talking went on. At last she spoke out.

'Would you mind taking the money please?' she enquired.

'I'm not just talking, you know, I'm showing her how to use the till!' was the reply.

'Perhaps it hasn't occurred to you,' Mrs Ashworth said sweetly, 'that if you don't serve the customers, very soon there'll be no need for *either* of you to use the till!'

'Oh – very sorry, I'm sure,' snarled the assistant, in a way which annoyed Mrs Ashworth very much. She paid for the products, received the bag and the till receipt in silence and walked out. It would be a very long time before she bought any more make-up from Booths again.

ACTIVITY 9

1 Discuss the attitude of the assistant who was teaching another girl to use the till. From the following list, write down the alternative which would have been the best way of dealing with Mrs Ashworth:

  a ignored Mrs Ashworth's request altogether
  b smile at Mrs Ashworth to let her know that she had been seen, but continue with the till training
  c leave the till training right away and serve Mrs Ashworth

2 What did Mrs Ashworth mean when she said '. . . there'll be no need for *either* of you to use the till!' Choose from:

  a the till training would be incomplete if it wasn't finished then

  b if customers were not served and didn't return, there would be no profit and the shop would close
  c she was telling them that she would complain to the manager

3 If *you* were the manager and received a complaint from Mrs Ashworth, what two actions would you take?

Choose from:

  1 write to Mrs Ashworth and apologise, stating what you were going to do to put the matter right
  2 decide that people would have to learn how to operate the till from an instruction booklet
  3 change all the tills in the shop to simple electronic ones

4 speak to the shop assistants about the importance of customers to the business and how to treat them

a 1 and 2
b 2 and 3
c 3 and 4
d 1 and 4

ACTIVITY 10

Work in a small group of 2–4 people.

You are going to collect and record data about customer satisfaction, by asking different people about their experiences.

1 Design a data collection sheet to find out if the person you speak to:

- has ever had a bad experience as a customer
- complained about the experience to the other person involved
- complained about the experience to the person's manager
- discussed the experience with family, friends or neighbours
- went to the shop (or place where the experience happened) again
- took any other action.

2 Try to obtain information from ten people each, to fill in your data collection sheet.

3 Add up the answers to each of the questions in your data record.

4 Describe the situation using *either* simple fractions (e.g. about a quarter of the people stated that they complained to the person's manager), *or* use percentages (e.g. about 25% of the people stated that they complained to the person's manager).

5 Check your records and your answers to make sure that they are accurate and complete.

CORE SKILLS: *Application of number 1.1 Collect and record data*

Ensuring health and safety

More and more customers know their rights and are quite likely to sue an organisation if they are injured owing to the carelessness of an employee. It is vital that staff should make a habit of keeping the workplace free from hazards. Litter should be picked up before someone slips on it, checks made on facilities to make sure they are safe. Hotels should have fire escapes, with signs pointing to the exits. Rooms should have a plan with exits marked clearly. Visitors to another country are usually advised to drink bottled water to save any problems and sometimes warned not to drink too much wine if they are not used to it, nor stay out in the sun all day long (even with protection).

Facilities should have clean kitchens and clean staff and emergency exits should be checked to make sure they are clear. Cleaning materials and chemicals (e.g. for use in a swimming pool) should be stored safely. Staff should have training in safety matters and should also be alert and responsible so that they can prevent problems arising.

Ensuring security

Security staff on duty in colleges, leisure centres, hotels, tourist attractions and recreation facilities help to make people feel more secure. Customers can also be encouraged not to carry too much cash with them, especially when they are in another country, and to use credit and debit cards as a safer form of payment. They should be told about areas which ought to be avoided. For security reasons, staff should wear identity badges.

Staff should have training to deal with people who shout at them or who threaten them with physical violence.

Information should be kept away from public view and access restricted to those who have a right to know. Intruder alarms can help to make stealing computers less likely. Customers are entitled to see any information about them which is held on computer and can ask to have any wrong information changed.

ACTIVITY 11

Write out the following sentences, filling in the missing word(s).

1 It is vital for staff to keep a workplace free from _____, otherwise customers may sue if they are injured.

2 Hotels should have fire _____ with signs pointing to emergency exits.

3 Bottled water will help to keep _____ to another country healthy.

4 Chemicals for use in a swimming pool should be _____ away safely.

5 Security staff help customers to feel more _____.

6 Information should be kept away from _____ view and access given only to those with a right to know.

7 Customers can ask to see data about themselves held on _____ and also ask for wrong information to be _____.

Communicating clearly and politely

ACTIVITY 12

Situation A

Work in pairs. Partner A works in the box office at a local theatre and Partner B is a customer. Partner A opens the conversation by asking for seats for ten people to see the Christmas show.

Partner B replies and tries to find out:

- what date is wanted
- if it is an afternoon or evening performance
- if any of the customers are entitled to concessionary seats (children, pensioners)
- which theatre seats are required – front stalls, back stalls, front circle, back circle, balcony.

The final decision is made for seats costing £15.00 with two concessionary seats at £8.00 each. Partner B works out the amount of money required.

Partner A points out that for ten seats a party booking reduction of 10% applies. Partner B works out the new figure.

Situation B

Change roles so that Partner B is now the customer and Partner A is an assistant in a local craft and gift shop. Partner B opens the conversation by asking for a suitable gift for a child.

Partner A replies and tries to find out:

- the child's gender
- the child's age
- the child's interests.

Partner A then makes appropriate suggestions for a gift.

Partner B makes a choice which costs £22.50.

Partner A says that there is a 10% reduction 'Special Offer' on this item and works out the correct price.

CORE SKILL: *Application of number 1.2 Tackle problems*
PC 1, 2, 3, 4
Range 1 – Technique: simple percentages of quantities

Customers often like to look round and think about the goods before they buy anything. They may decide not to make a purchase on that occasion, but since they have seen what a retail outlet has to offer, it is very likely that they will return at some future date. It is important not to pressure these customers. Smile to show that you have noticed them. If they want to buy something, they will approach you.

People looking round a travel agency often have an idea of what they want to do for a holiday and may like to have brochures given and suggested places to visit given to them. The trained salesperson has to judge the moment.

Remember to use 'please' and 'thank you' in your dealings with customers. 'Do you need any help?' is often appropriate; the customer can respond 'yes' or 'no' to this without feeling pushed into buying something. Taking extra trouble to find exactly what the customer wants and offering to order something in the right size, are polite and pleasant ways of making sure that the customer will want to return.

Politeness when using the telephone can include asking customers for their telephone numbers if the call is a complaint, or likely to take a long time, and ringing them back immediately.

ACTIVITY 13

Telephone talk

Look at the following remarks made on the telephone. Write them out and then write your own, polite version, alongside.

1 Hang on a minute.

2 He's not here.

3 Yer wot?

4 She's in a meeting.

5 I can't hear you.

6 There's nobody here but me.

Don't forget the use of body language when you are communicating politely. Facial gestures, drumming your fingers, looking round when someone is talking and frowning will signal to the customer that you are not interested in what they have to say.

Dealing with problems

Organisations have realised that it costs five times as much to gain a new customer as it does to keep an existing one, so more attention is now being paid to the minority of customers who complain, to try to put matters right. Many people simply do not bother to complain and go somewhere else for their goods and services. It has been found that customers who *do* complain and then are satisfied with the way in which the complaint has been dealt with, are more loyal than customers who never complain.

It is important to treat any complaints promptly and to resolve them as quickly as possible. Common causes of complaint are apparent rudeness of employees (who may not know that this is how they appear) and limited choices in sizes and styles of clothing. Customers also complain if their expectations are not satisfied.

If you are dealing with a complaint, take a note of the customer's name, address and telephone number. Take notes of the complaint and read them back to make sure you have understood the problem. Tell the customer what you are going to do about it – tell your supervisor, exchange the goods, make a refund. If it is not a problem you can deal with, contact the correct person *immediately*. If someone is complaining by telephone, do not keep them hanging on but offer to ring back.

If you have an angry customer who uses unacceptable language, ask your supervisor to deal with him or her. Keep calm; complaints are not meant for you personally!

Your questions may show that the customer has not followed instructions or has not understood an explanation. Put this right tactfully: 'There has been a misunderstanding . . .' *not* 'You've got it all wrong!'

Agree on a solution and then do it. If you have several complaints about the same thing, tell your supervisor as there may be a larger problem here. After the problem has been solved, check up to see if the customer is satisfied with the result.

ACTIVITY 14

Work in a small group of 2 to 4 people and discuss the following problems with each other.

When you have decided on a solution, write a short account of how the matter should be dealt with.

1 **Problem with a product** A customer brings a riding hat back to the shop where it was bought and explains that it does not fit the child for whom it was bought. The shop assistant is not sure if the customer is entitled to money back – after all, the product is not 'fit for the purpose for which it was sold', or does that mean that the riding hat itself must have no faults? Should the assistant suggest that the customer comes back with the child and the hat will then be exchanged for one which is the correct size?

<u>2</u> **Problem with a service** Two customers take a coach trip to see a stately home and have booked a tour which includes the services of a guide. They were not very happy with the tour as there were a great many people in the group and they could not hear the guide. At the end of the tour, they complained that they had no information about the stately home and they were not happy with the service. As it was the last tour of the day, it was not possible to ask them to join the next one. Should the person dealing with the complaint offer money back? Should the coach company offer another trip some time in the future? Should an apology be offered?

<u>3</u> **Problem with a facility** A couple and two women friends had each booked a room in a particular hotel in Majorca as part of a holiday put together by a tour operator. On arriving at the hotel, they were all told that there had been a mistake and there were no rooms available. Although the two sets of customers were complete strangers to each other, the hotel manager offered them the use of an apartment to share. Should they complain to the manager? Should they inform the tour operator's representative? Should they refuse to share and ask for other arrangements to be made? Would they be entitled to compensation because of the problem with the facility?

<u>4</u> **Problem with own ability to deliver effective customer service** People who complain may ask to see the manager, which can make the person trying to give service feel that they are not competent. The customer may ask for something you do not know about. It is a good idea to say that you will bring someone who is more senior or more expert on the subject to see the customer. This will make the customer feel that the complaint or request is being dealt with by the best person. If you are faced with someone who insists on speaking to the manager, should you try to find out what it is about? Should you call the manager at once and say it is urgent? Should you tell the customer that someone will contact them at home?

<u>5</u> **Problem with unreasonable customer expectations** Most people understand the expression 'you get what you pay for', but there are times when customers have unreasonable expectations. It is important to keep such a person away from the other customers (complaints are catching) until you have thought of a solution. If a customer complains that a cheap seat in the theatre meant that he or she was not able to see the stage properly, should you write and apologise? Should you suggest that other customers sitting there have never complained? Should you point out that there is a much better view from the more expensive stalls?

Jobs in leisure and tourism

The following information is intended to help the role-plays which follow by giving some background information on the types of jobs available in the leisure and tourism industry.

Read the information through *slowly* before you attempt the activities which follow.

Souvenir shop assistant

Salma is interested in history, and when she left school the chance came for her to take up a shop assistant's post in the souvenir shop at a nearby historic house.

She discovered that tourists like to know about the souvenirs they are buying, so she found out something of the history of the house and can now relate this to the products in the shop. She makes personal contact with the customers, and is always happy to tell them more about which of the goods on offer are made locally and relate this to craft skills in the area.

Salma takes the money, uses the till, gives a receipt and the change and puts the purchase in a bag, as she would do if she was employed in a retail shop in the High Street. She also tidies up the stock when the visitors have gone, notes which goods are running low and re-orders them, as well as noticing which products seem to interest visitors most.

She sells quality goods, items which have been produced using craft skills, unusual products which cannot be bought anywhere else, and preserves which have been made locally. She has stocks of homemade fudge and toffee which does not cost a lot to buy, because many children visit the attraction and want something to take home to their families.

Salma also has to keep watch when large groups of people visit the shop to make sure that no-one takes anything without paying for it. She looks into the mirrors (which are positioned so that she can see into corners when she is at the till) and challenges people who are on their way out with unpaid goods by asking, 'Do you want to pay for that?'

She works at weekends, when it is busy. Some historic houses are only open at certain times of the year, but this particular one is open all year round. This means Salma's job is a permanent one.

Waiter or waitress

Christine's first job as a waitress was at a big hotel in the months leading up to Christmas. She was told that it was a part-time, temporary job, and that when January came there would be no work. She was trained on the job and had to help to clean the premises, set up the tables and place the chairs tidily before the customers arrived. The Head Waiter told her what to do and at first she helped another trained waitress. Christine had the manual skill necessary for the job and, after some practice, worked as a Silver Service waitress, putting the food on to customers' plates at the table. She liked to see the experienced waiters cooking special dishes at the customers' tables and was interested in the work of the Wine Waitress, who offered advice on various wines to customers asking her opinion.

When her contract came to an end, Christine applied for part-time work in the evening and at weekends in the banqueting suite of the local leisure centre, and is hoping to get a full-time position when she leaves college.

One of Christine's fellow students works as a waitress in a café in the town centre at weekends. She finds this is very different to Christine's work, as the people she serves are in a hurry to go back to their shopping. At peak times (such as in summer or December) she has to serve people very quickly, so that the café can meet its target of customer numbers it expects to process.

Ride operator in a theme park

Winston enjoys his work in the theme park where there are lots of rides for the public. He can find himself doing anything from helping children slide down chutes, to making sure people are safely strapped in for a wild ride on The Big One.

Winston doesn't need to take the customers' money as they pay an 'all in' fee to come into the theme park. He makes sure people are comfortable and safe, and looks after groups of people (such as the elderly or special needs) who may need help getting on to the rides.

People look forward to having a good time on their day out and Winston helps them to do this, although sometimes he feels as if he has been smiling at thousands as he welcomes them on to the ride. He has good communication skills and is very fit. He has been trained to know what to do in an emergency and knows how most of the rides work. He enjoys working in the open air and takes pride in keeping his ride well-maintained, clean, safe and tidy.

Hotel receptionist

Michelle had to wait until she was 18 until she could apply for a job as a hotel receptionist, as the desk had to be covered 24 hours a day and this meant working shifts.

Michelle is the first person the guests see and so she must always have a good appearance and a friendly manner. She receives the guests and books them in, answers their queries and tells them how to get to their rooms. She operates a computer system for the bookings, which is also used for making reservations and printing out accounts at the end of the visitor's stay. She may have to deal with people who arrive without booking in and cope with decisions about rooms booked for people who do not turn up. Sometimes a tour representative will arrive with a large group whose rooms have to be sorted and luggage dealt with quickly. She often feels that one pair of hands is not enough when she is answering the telephone, dealing with several guests who have just arrived, and replying to the housekeeper's query. She speaks a little French and Spanish, which helps when visitors from abroad arrive. She needs a good telephone manner, plenty of patience and the ability to keep calm.

Tour representative

When holiday-makers arrive in a strange country on a package tour, perhaps unable to speak the language, they are welcomed by a tour representative who works for the tour operator. They are taken to their holiday accommodation and settled in.

Adam works in the UK for an American tour operator. He meets his party of Americans at the airport, directs them to the coach and stays with them for the time they are touring the UK. As they approach each historical building or heritage site, Adam tells the group what they are about to see. He has worked out in advance where the coach will stop for a drink and toilet break and will keep the group together so that they don't spend too much time when they stop.

Adam works long hours on the days when he is conducting a tour. He offers his clients help and advice and is available to help with any problem and difficulty. Adam has excellent communication skills, stamina, good health and is able to organise paperwork and solve problems. He can speak two other languages and has knowledge of different cultural backgrounds so that he can help visitors when necessary.

Travel agency clerk

Most of the work in travel is in this country, not abroad. People travel by road, rail, ship or aeroplane and there are jobs in all these areas.

Paul is a travel agency clerk. If individuals do not want to work out all the details of their travel, or if they want a holiday package, they usually go to a travel agency. Paul has worked in his job for three years and has now passed the ABTA examinations. In his job he may be asked to make ferry bookings; work out the best way to go to Australia by air with two stopovers and hotel accommodation; book family seats on a local coach going to a theme park in the long school break; and sort out a package holiday for a family whose first choice is booked up.

He knows about travel insurance, passports, visas, any inoculations needed before visitors can enter certain countries, foreign currency exchange rates, and can issue travellers' cheques and help with car-hire bookings. He may have to contact a network of suppliers to put together a special package for a client. He makes arrangements for business travellers, works out scheduled flights which will get the traveller to the right destination, books accommodation and arranges to have a hire car waiting at the airport.

Paul knows about the 24-hour clock, has a good knowledge of geography and can work well under pressure. He can operate a computer, likes dealing with people, has an excellent telephone manner and can stay calm under pressure.

The activity produces your **Evidence indicator**. This is a record of you providing a service to customers in six different customer service situations and is assessed by your tutor. Three situations are placed in the leisure and recreation industry, where you will role-play a souvenir shop assistant, a waiter or waitress, and a ride operator in a theme park. In the travel and tourism context, you will play a hotel receptionist, a tour representative and a travel agency clerk. In each situation you will be asked to identify service needs, provide effective customer service, and communicate with and solve problems for all the customers in the range.

Evidence indicator

Each person in the group should play the role of a staff member once in each situation, so that everyone can be assessed as they deal with their customers. When the 'staff member' is happy with their role-play, it can then be evaluated by the assessor (probably your tutor) who will be checking up on:

- how the student identified the service needs of the customer
- how effective service to customers was provided
- whether communication was clear and polite
- whether any problems were dealt with effectively
- whether the role-player called in a more experienced 'member of staff' if this was appropriate for the situation.

After each situation has been completed by everyone in the group, students should write a short evaluation of their own role as a staff member, stating what preparations were made for the role-play (reading, observation, work experience) and what improvements might be made.

The situations may be recorded on video for assessment.

Situation A – groups of customers

1 Work in groups of 5 to 6 people. Two people play the role of shop assistant in a souvenir shop at a historic house, heritage centre or museum. The rest of the students play a group of people who come into the shop together at the end of a tour of the facility. Their roles are:

- to enquire if an item (e.g. jam, toys, pottery) is handmade locally
- to ask about the candle-making demonstration and then complain when they find it has been cancelled
- to try to shoplift when the assistants are busy elsewhere
- to enquire whether dried flower arrangements can be ordered and how long the order would take.

Each shop assistant should deal with two customers.

2 The same situation is repeated with two other people as shop assistants and students playing the parts of a group of customers. Their roles are:

- to enquire if wool sweaters can be made to measure by local craftspeople

- to ask the whereabouts of the café and then complain that they have been there already but only soup and a roll were served for lunch
- to try to shoplift while the assistants are occupied
- to browse among the items but not buy anything.

3 The last two people in the group play the shop assistants and the other students act as the group of customers. Their roles are:

- to enquire if there are any part-time jobs to be had at the facility
- to complain that the facility is closed on Mondays
- to try to shoplift while the assistants are occupied
- to ask the assistants to cash a cheque, although the customer does not have any identification.

Situation B – customers with special needs; dealing with complaints

1 Work in groups of 3 to 4 people. The person playing the staff member is a waiter or waitress in a restaurant to which the other people have come for a meal. They role-play:

- a person who is a wheelchair user and needs the restaurant chair to be moved in order to sit at the table
- a person who immediately wants a drink of water before ordering anything
- a person who knows the waiter or waitress and tries to detain him or her by talking too long.

2 Change the member of staff; the other students role-play:

- a person who has impaired hearing and who wishes to see the menu but cannot hear the waiter or waitress
- a person who reads the menu and is critical to staff about the prices
- a person who cannot make up his or her mind when everyone else has ordered and is waiting impatiently.

3 Change the member of staff; the other students role-play:

- a person who cannot read and needs help from the waiter or waitress
- a person who is in a hurry
- a person who complains that the last time he or she was here, the soup was cold.

4 Change the member of staff; the other students role-play:

- a person with his or her right arm in a sling who needs special cutlery
- a person who complains he or she is sitting in a draught
- a person who insists on asking 'who's on in the kitchen today?' and then asks if that person is a good chef.

Situation C – customers of different ages

1 Work in groups of 3 to 4 people The staff member plays the role of a ride operator in a theme park. There is a height restriction on this particular ride: everyone has to be at least 1.5m tall and there is a measuring stand with the height marked on it before the customer gets on the ride. Other roles are:

- a young person *under* 1.5m tall who very much wants to ride
- an adult who complains that the admission price to the theme park includes rides but the queues for each ride are too long
- a teenager who wants you to stop the ride when it reaches the top so that he or she can look round the park for the water chute.

The staff member deals with the situations in ways that try to achieve customer satisfaction.

2 Change to another member of staff: the rest of the group play the following roles:

- a child who has lost his or her school party and needs help
- an older adult who insists on going on the ride but is too small, but insists that the height restriction does not apply to adults
- a teenager who has just lost the pre-paid ticket but points out that he or she must have had one to get into the theme park in the first place.

The staff member deals with the situations in ways that try to achieve customer satisfaction.

3 Re-play the situations until every member of the group has had a turn of playing the part of the staff member.

Situation D – customers who do not speak English

1 Work in groups of 3 to 4 people. Take turns to play the part of a hotel receptionist, who is at the reception desk when a group of people who do not speak English approach. It may be necessary for the receptionist to obtain more experienced help if the difficulties cannot be solved.

The students playing the non-English speaking people try to find out:

- where the restaurant is
- what time it opens for the evening meal
- when it closes.

2 Change the member of staff, and the non-English speaking students try to:

- order a foreign newspaper
- order a cup of tea *now*
- order a taxi in an hour's time.

3 Change the member of staff until every member of the group has tried the role of the hotel receptionist.

Situation E – customers from different cultural backgrounds

1 Work in groups of 3 to 4 people. The person playing the member of staff is a tour representative, who is dealing with customers from a different cultural background who have come on holiday to the UK. Other members of the group play the part of the customers just booked into a hotel; they require the representative to obtain for them:

- a private sitting room to be used by ladies only
- vegetarian meals
- non-alcoholic drinks with their meals.

2 Change the member of staff, who now plays a tour representative in another country. The other students play visitors on a coach trip who are not wearing appropriate clothing for visiting churches and cathedrals. The staff member has to persuade:

- a man to wear something over his scant T-shirt
- a woman to wear something on her head

* teenagers to cover their legs up.

If possible explain that their dress would be considered disrespectful.

3 Change the person playing the member of staff until everyone has had a turn.

Situation F – individual customers

Work in pairs. Partner A plays the role of a travel agency clerk first and Partner B is the customer, and then they change over.

Partner A
Partner B opens the conversation by saying that he or she wants to book a holiday for a family with three children (ages 6, 8 and 11) in the UK. Partner A asks some questions to find out:

* if transport is needed
* whether the family prefer self-catering or want a hotel
* if they like organised holidays or prefer to organise themselves
* what price range is being considered
* any hobbies or interests which need to be taken into account.

Partner A also asks any other questions which will help to pinpoint the kind of holiday the customer is looking for. Partner A could then make some suggestions.

Partner B
Partner A opens the conversation by saying that he or she wants to book a long weekend break in a city in the UK and would like some suggestions. Partner B asks some questions to find out:

* if transport is needed
* whether it is to be a hotel or self-catering
* how many people will be going
* if they want a 'theme' holiday
* what price range is being considered
* any interests (such as theatres, music venues, history or heritage) which need to be taken into account.

Partner B also asks any other questions which will help to pinpoint the kind of holiday the customer is looking for. Partner B could then make some suggestions.

The assessor will add an evaluation of the way each student meets the performance criteria and satisfies the expectations of the customer. The work is graded on two themes: **planning** and **information seeking and information handling**. In addition **evaluation** and **quality of outcome** are also graded. Video recordings may be used as evidence.

Evaluation

Look back at the work you have done for this unit:

- check that you have done everything you were asked to do
- look at the method you used
- look at other methods which you decided not to use
- what were the good things about the method you used?
- what were the bad things about the methods which you did not use?
- have you any ideas about the way in which the work could have been improved?

Write a short statement headed 'Evaluation'.

Revision and specimen test questions

Focus 3: Providing service for customers

Reference: Element 1.2 PC1, PC2

External test requirements

a *Identify service needs of different customers in given customer service situations.*

Range

Customer service needs: for information, for advice, for assistance

Providing information for the customer is one of the main jobs in providing a service. You may make suggestions and offer leaflets, brochures, notices, prices and times of leisure classes, either from a card index or from a computer file.

1 A hotel reception will provide information about local places of interest by:
   a having a tour guide on duty during the day
   b keeping leaflets and brochures on a stand in reception
   c asking the staff to suggest places of interest to guests
   d declaring there is nothing of interest locally

2 A customer who wants to know the cheapest ferry fare to Europe from the UK would ask advice from:
   a Le Shuttle
   b friends who always fly to their holiday destination

c a merchant shipping company
   d a travel agent

3 Eureka! museum for children now have audio guides to exhibits, to be used by visitors who need assistance because they are:
   a partially sighted
   b hearing impaired
   c wheelchair users
   d slow learners

Range

Customer service needs for a specific product/service, for selling, coaching, running outdoor activities, making bookings, serving food and drinks, for a prompt service

4 A tennis coach is asked by one of the students for advice on which tennis racquet would be the best one to use. The coach will suggest:
   a the most expensive racquet
   b the best racquet for the job the student can afford
   c any racquet will do as long as it's lightweight
   d a coach's job is to teach the sport, not advise on racquets

5 A party of older people wish to take a holiday where they can be transported through the countryside, look at historical and heritage sites and stay in hotels in different locations within the UK. A travel agent dealing with them would be most likely to suggest that their needs would be met by:
   a staying for a week near a National Trust house

b taking a holiday in a hotel reached by steps with a view

c going on a package tour of the vineyards of Portugal

d taking a History and Heritage coach tour in the UK

6 A customer enquires about holding a children's Pool Party using the swimming pool and balcony of the local swimming baths. The customer needs:

a to make an appointment to speak to the manager

b the receptionist to give information and make the booking

c to provide his or her own life-guards for the party

d to be told that only good swimmers should join the party

7 A family group celebrates a special birthday in a restaurant. Their service needs would best be met by:

a the waiter or waitress offering them the menu

b the waiter or waitress offering congratulations but not serving them

c finding the place was so busy that they would have to wait

d being told that there was no special treatment for birthdays

External test requirements

b *Recognise how to provide effective customer service to different customers in given customer service situations.*

Range

Effective customer service: meeting customers' needs, ensuring health and safety (of customers, of self, of colleagues, of facility)

It is important to keep the workplace free from danger, reporting anything which is a hazard, having signs to show fire escape routes and emergency exits. Kitchens should be clean. Chemicals should be stored away and staff should know what to do if anyone splashes their eyes, skin or clothing with chemicals.

8 A leisure assistant cleans the tiled reception area with water and a mop. A 'wet floor' notice stand should be placed in the area when:

a the work is finished

b the work is half done

c as the work begins

d ten minutes before the work starts

9 Children in a school party visiting a museum are anxious to get to the exhibits in the next room. Which behaviour would the gallery attendant ask them to stop because it would be the most dangerous?

a shouting as they walk

b running along the corridor

c standing on tip-toe

d marching along singing

Range

Effective customer service: ensuring security of customers, of self, of colleagues, of facility, of information

Measures to help people to feel secure are to have security guards on duty, to encourage people to use credit and debit cards instead of carrying a lot of cash and to tell people about dangerous areas in a location.

Burglar and fire alarms help to keep a facility secure. Information should be kept where only people with the right to know can see it and not left on view for anyone to see.

10 A party of holiday-makers would feel more secure if the tour representative explained:

a the rate of exchange they could expect for their money

b how to order a meal in a foreign language

c the shortest way into the local town centre

d where the local drug-dealers operate

11 A conference organiser using a hotel has details of delegates in a file on her desk in the entrance hall. She is called away to the telephone in another room. Before leaving, she should:

a lock the file in a safe at the other end of the corridor

b leave the closed file on the desk

c quickly put the file in the unlocked drawer of her desk

d close the file and take it with her

Focus 4: Dealing with customers

Reference: Element 1.2 PC3, PC4

External test requirements

a *Recognise how to communicate clearly and politely with different customers in given customer service situations.*

Range

Communicate face-to-face, in writing, on the telephone. Clearly: to ensure that customers understand the message, to clarify own understanding of customers' wishes. Politely: in a manner appropriate to the customer, in a manner appropriate to the situation. Customers: individuals, groups, of different ages, from different cultural backgrounds, non-English speaking, with specific needs

When communicating face-to-face or by telephone, staff should ask questions, then repeat the answers to the customer. It is useful to take notes and then read them back to make sure that staff have understood the customer.

Letters or memos should be easy to understand, short, polite with no errors. The final sentence or paragraph should state what the writer wants the reader to do. The tone should suit the situation and the particular customer.

12 A customer in a souvenir shop has been looking round for such a long time that the assistant wonders whether there is going to be a theft. Which of the following would be the best thing for the assistant to say to the customer?

a Have you any idea what you want?

b We're closing in a minute.

c Can you please hurry?

d May I help you?

13 The booking clerk in a car-hire firm receives a telephone request for a car to be available to meet a visitor at the airport on the island of Jersey. Which two of the following should the clerk do before ending the telephone call?

1 remark on the beauty of Jersey

2 ask if the visitor has ever been to Guernsey

3 read back the details of the car hire

4 check the spelling of the visitor's name

Choose from:

a 1 and 2

b 2 and 3

c 3 and 4

d 1 and 4

External test requirements

b *Recognise how to deal effectively with problems in given customer service situations.*

Range

Problems: with product/service, with facility, with own ability to deliver effective customer service, with unreasonable customer expectations. Deal effectively: meeting service needs of customers whenever possible, referring to the appropriate person whenever required

Organisations know that to keep customers they must solve problems and resolve complaints. Staff should take notes of the customer's name, address and telephone number and the complaint. It should be read back to the customer to make sure that it has been understood correctly. If the member of staff cannot solve the problem, someone who can do so should be contacted immediately. A solution should be agreed on if possible and then put into operation. Afterwards, a check should be made to see that the customer is satisfied.

14 A souvenir shop assistant sells homemade chocolate fudge to two school children. They go outside the shop, open it and find that the chocolate has white heat marks on it. They bring it back and complain. Which of the following should the shop assistant do?
   a tell them it is a heat mark and the chocolate is all right
   b say that the firm never exchanges chocolate
   c apologise, explain the reason for the mark and offer an exchange
   d refuse to change it because children have no customer rights

15 A new waiter finds himself very busy and overhears a group of people at one of his tables grumbling because the service is slow. Which of the following would solve the problem of his not being able to deliver effective customer service?
   a try to work more quickly

   b ask another waiter who is not busy to serve that table
   c complain to the manager that he has too much to do
   d tell himself that the group will just have to wait

16 A general operator in a theme park is working on a ride which has a height restriction. A young boy objects strongly when the operator says he is not tall enough, as his friend, who is younger but taller, has been allowed on the ride. The customer is being unreasonable as the height restriction is quite clear. Which of the following would be the most likely solution to the problem?
   a the operator diverts the customer by suggesting another ride
   b the operator states that the rule can't be broken
   c the operator tells the boy that he is very small for his age
   d the operator argues with the boy about the rule

17 A hotel receptionist finds a large queue at her desk after a number of guests arrive all at once. Which of the following would be the best way to handle the problem and meet the needs of the customers?
   a get annoyed with the tour representative who has brought them
   b deal with the first guests and ignore the rest
   c grumble that she only has one pair of hands
   d smile, say 'I'll be with you in a minute' and work through the queue

18 A tour representative finds that one of the holiday-makers has hurt her leg badly getting on to the airport bus. Which of the following would meet the needs of the customers most effectively?

a leave the group and take the injured lady to a doctor

b tell the lady that first-aid is available at the hotel

c arrange for the injured lady to go to hospital and then deal with the rest of the group

d keep everyone waiting and send for the airport manager

Maintain customer records

Part of customer service is to demonstrate a caring attitude to other members of staff and to help each other when required to do so. Those students who have had some work experience will have had to call upon an appropriate person, a supervisor or a colleague with more experience or with specific skills, to help them with a problem. This caring attitude to other staff can be developed by giving help to fellow students when working through realistic simulations.

In order to obtain examples of customer records, students are asked to take the part of customers and of members of leisure and tourism staff so that they can simulate situations and cover the range required.

Observations made through work experience, work shadowing or as a customer of a leisure and tourism organisation may be used to supplement the activities which follow. Some students may be able to obtain actual forms to use for recording customer information.

Types of customer records

Customer information may be kept on computer or in a paper-based system. All filing systems are in alphabetical order, but may also be in geographical or subject order as well. It is important to file work properly so that it can be retrieved when it is needed. A note should be made in one file if the actual document is in another file, e.g. a letter may be under a *subject* heading and a note made in the *geographical* file. Information used for customer records is usually name, address and telephone number and the appropriate financial details.

It is important to file work properly so that it can be retrieved easily.

Read through the rest of this chapter and decide how you are going to tackle it. Make an action plan. Where there are forms to word process or to copy, the group may decide to divide the work between them. In some cases, the person playing the part of a staff member may have to seek out information to give to the 'customer' in a situation.

When you have completed a situation in which you were the staff member, you should evaluate it against what you were asked to do. If you think of any improvements afterwards, record these in your evaluation. Your simulations should be observed by an assessor, so keep your tutor informed of your plan of action and arrange for assessment when you are ready for it.

Some sales are recorded on an electronic till. Electronic tills print out details such as: the shop name and address, the manager's name, the name of the assistant at the cash point, the day, date and time the goods were bought, and an itemised list of all the purchases and their cost.

Other tills print a simple receipt showing the cost, the money handed over and the change given. If the till is a manual one, it will not print a receipt and the assistant will have to write one out. This receipt will look something like this:

HERITAGE HOUSE CRAFT SHOP
Grange Park
CHESTER

Received from...

the sum of ....

for ....

Date..

SIGNED ....

🏃 🏃 🏃 🏃 🏃 **ACTIVITY 1** 🏃 🏃 🏃 🏃 🏃

Situation A – sales records

Work with a group of 3 to 4 people.

1 Obtain information about the kinds of items sold in gift and craft shops. You may try reference books such as *Yellow Pages* ('The Inside Guide') or your tourist information centre for ideas on the kinds of goods sold.

As a group, list about 20 of these items and put them on a stock list, using word processing if possible. Make a copy of the stock list for each member of the group and save it on disk.

2 Word process or type some receipts (as shown above). In turn, role-play the part of

an assistant in a gift or craft shop, with other students acting as customers, and buy one of the items suggested on the stock list. When the 'customer' has chosen an item, write out a receipt for it. Keep a copy of all the receipts written out for your own records.

3 After you have issued the receipts, bring up the stock list on computer and alter it, so that it now shows present stock levels minus the items which have just been bought. Print out a copy of this stock list and keep it with your original list and your copies of the receipts.

4 When the last person in the group has printed out the stock list, discuss which items were the most popular buys and which were unpopular with your particular group. Discuss the reasons for this – did the age of the customers have anything to do with their preferences? Word process a short account of your findings and attach it to your other items.

Ask your assessor to observe your simulations when you are ready to carry out this activity.

Keep your records and your observer's comments for your **Evidence indicator**.

CORE SKILL: *Information Technology 1.1 Prepare information*
Range 1, 2, 3, 4, 5

A small business uses a card index to keep records of enquiries and orders. Cards are usually approximately 16.2 cm × 11.4 cm and are stored in a small metal filing drawer in alphabetical order. Sometimes subject order is also used (i.e. anniversary, birthday, celebration); this is also in alphabetical order.

ACTIVITY 2

Situation B – enquiry details

Work in groups of 3 to 4 people.

A restaurant offers a special private function room to customers who want a private party. Enquiry details are recorded on card index which looks like this:

ENQUIRY
GRANGE PARK RESTAURANT
Fieldgate
CHESTER

FUNCTION _____

NAME OF CUSTOMER _____

ADDRESS _____

TELEPHONE NUMBER _____

DATE _____ TIME _____

APPROXIMATE PRICE PER HEAD _____

OTHER DETAILS _____

---

1 Word process four cards 'landscape' way on A4 paper. Photocopy on to card and make eight cards altogether, of the size used in a card-index file.

2 In turn, each person acts as assistant manager, taking enquiry details on a card for a special function. Other students act as customers making the enquiry. Customers choose a function from: anniversary, birthday party, christening party, celebration party, engagement party, office annual party, retirement party or wedding.

When the assistant manager has completed the cards, they are sorted into alphabetical order of the functions.

3 Assume that one of the customers has telephoned to say that the enquiry is now a definite order. Each student chooses one enquiry card to use for the details and word processes a letter to that customer confirming that the order has been received.

In the first paragraph, begin 'We refer to your enquiry . . .' In the second paragraph, say that the order has been received and a definite booking has been made. Ask for a deposit of £25.00. In the last paragraph, ask the customer to telephone a week before the function to give the exact number of people attending.

4 Evaluate your work. Were there any difficulties or problems which could have been solved before you began? Were there any improvements which could have been made? Write a short account of your evaluation. Add to your card-index records and your letter to the customer.

Arrange for your simulation to be assessed and add the observer's comments to the work you have done for this activity. Keep it all together to use for your **Evidence indicator**.

Situation C – records of complaints

When a complaint is made, there is often a ready-made form to be filled in. The person complaining (the complainant) need not get angry or upset; most organisations are only too pleased to put complaints right and keep their customers happy! A complaint form may be similar to the one shown on the next page:

GRANGE PARK LEISURELAND
COMPLAINT FORM

NAME OF COMPLAINANT _____

ADDRESS _____

TELEPHONE NUMBER _____

DATE OF INCIDENT OR COMPLAINT _____

DETAILS OF COMPLAINT

DETAILS TAKEN BY _____

DATED _____

SIGNED (MEMBER OF STAFF) _____

SIGNED (COMPLAINANT) _____

🏃 🏃 🏃 🏃 🏃 **ACTIVITY 3** 🏃 🏃 🏃 🏃 🏃

Work with a group of 3 to 4 people.

1 Word process a complaint form (as shown above) and print two copies for each member of the group.

2 In turn, act as the staff member at a theme park taking down details of a complaint from customers. Show sympathy to customers and assure them that their complaints will be dealt with promptly, but do not blame anyone or accept responsibility.

You may use your own ideas or choose from the following.

▶ The complainant has paid to come into the theme park and used all the facilities, but states that since six rides are out of action, he/she has not had value for money and suggests that the situation is against the Trades Description Act.

▶ The complainant was told that there was a café at all times, but today it was locked and barred. As a consequence a whole family has had nothing to eat and the day's outing has been spoiled.

▶ The complainant has come especially to see the Baby Animal Zoo which was advertised in the leaflet and is very annoyed to find that it no longer exists. The customer wants his or her money back.

- The locking bar on a seat on one of the rides was loose and the complainant had been thrown about and bruised an arm.
- The discount coupon on the leaflet has not been accepted at the admission gate because the complainant did not have proof of identity, but does not think this should be necessary as no mention is made on the leaflet.
- The 'free' ride on the train round the theme park applied only to those people who bought a ticket for Marineland, but this was not made clear on the brochure and the complainant objects to extra charges.
- A wheelchair user in the complainant's party could not get down the path to see the sea lions because the steps did not have a ramp at the side which could be used.
- The Water Splash went wrong and the complainant's whole party was soaked. There was nowhere to dry off.

Keep a copy of the complaint form you filled in. More than one complaint can be dealt with if you wish.

3 Evaluate the complaint form. Was there enough space for all the necessary information? Did you need any more details? Look back on the way in which you dealt with the complaint and suggest any possible improvements.

4 Arrange for your simulation to be assessed.

Keep a copy of your complaint form, your evaluation and the observations of your assessor and use them for your **Evidence indicator**.

CORE SKILL: *Communication 1.2 Produce written material*
Range 1, 2, 3 (pre-set format), 4
Information Technology 1.1 Prepare information
Range 1, 2, 3, 4, 5

A **memorandum** is a note which is sent from one department or one branch in a firm to another. It is different from a letter because it has no 'Dear Sir' and no 'Yours faithfully'. Instead, it has pre-printed information to fill in stating the date, who it is to and from, and sometimes a reference. The 'to' and 'from' lines can be filled in with the names of the staff or their titles (such as 'Personnel Officer' or 'Sports Supervisor').

Memos (the short word for memoranda) are sent for the following reasons:

- to make a request
- to give information
- to persuade someone to do something

Memos are usually factual in tone. Slang and local words are not used in memos, which may have to go to people higher in the organisation than your own level, to people on the same level or to people below you.

Health and safety of colleagues

You are the Office Junior in the Human Resources Department (this is the department which deals with staff matters and is sometimes called the Personnel Department). Your Human Resources Officer has received the following memo which is shown to you:

MEMORANDUM

TO   Human Resources Officer
FROM   Sales Supervisor
DATE   19 November (this year)

I have been approached by several of the Sales Staff who have requested breaks from their job every hour and a half and have also stated that they are eligible for eyetests paid for by the firm as they use a display screen in the course of their work.

Would you please let me know if this is necessary?

The Human Resources Officer asks you to obtain information about the use of display screen equipment and reply to the above memo with the information you consider to be relevant. The following information is given but is not in the logical order you will need for your reply.

You have discovered that the Sales Staff use the display screen to answer certain queries from customers, but they do not work intensively on the display screen and frequently leave it to do other work, such as finding suitable information and giving it to the customer. However, they spend as much as three or more hours using the display screen.

Look at the following information and write a memo from yourself, Office Junior, to the Human Resources Officer.

Health and safety information for display screen users

1 People who use display screen equipment must have health and safety training in the use of any workstation they may be required to work.

2 The user's employer must provide eye and eyesight tests and pay for them. They must also provide and pay for spectacles, but they can choose the firm who carries out the tests.

3 Display screen jobs should be mixed with other work to prevent the worker from being tired.

4 If the job is all display screen work, breaks must be given.

5 Short, frequent breaks are best, for example, 5–10 minute breaks every hour.

6 Users should be able to choose when to take breaks after they have been given information and training on the need for breaks.

7 Examples of display screen users include people who work on a display screen unit for more than three hours daily, e.g. data input operator, word-processing worker, secretary.

8 Health problems can result from poor organisation of work, poor posture and bad working environment. Problems can be prevented by good design of the workplace and worker training.

CORE SKILL: *Communication 1.2 Produce written material*
PC 1, 2, 3, 4
Range 1, 2, 3 (pre-set format), 4

ACTIVITY 5

Situation D – customer registration

Work in groups of 3 to 4 people.

Visitors staying in a hotel in the UK are asked to fill in a form which is used to register them as guests.

1 Make duplicates of the following Guest Registration Form.

2 Each person takes it in turn to be the hotel receptionist. The other students play the part of hotel guests and fill in a registration form. The person playing the part of the receptionist collects the forms.

THE HERITAGE HOTEL
Grange Park Lane
Fieldgate
CHESTER
CH1 3DY

GUEST REGISTRATION FORM

SURNAME_____INITIALS _____

ARRIVAL DATE_____DEPARTURE DATE_____

HOME ADDRESS _____

_____

_____

TELEPHONE NO_____

METHOD OF PAYMENT (PLEASE TICK) _____CAR REG NO _____

CASH_____CHEQUE_____ACCOUNT TO COMPANY_____CREDIT CARD _____

SIGNATURE_____

---

3 From the details on the form, the receptionist should allocate a room number to each guest and put the following information on computer:

- name and address
- arrival date
- actual arrival time
- departure date
- deposit
- account to be settled by
- reservation booked by
- room number
- rate.

ACTIVITY 6

Situation E – request sheets

Work in groups of 3 to 4 people.

A hotel is offering cut-price weekend breaks from Saturday lunch time until afternoon tea on Sunday. This includes up to two Sunday newspapers delivered to the guests' rooms.

The receptionist asks guests to request their choice of Sunday newspaper when they book in by filling in a form.

1 Take two copies of the following Request Sheet for each person in the group.

THE HERITAGE HOTEL
Grange Park Lane
Fieldgate
CHESTER
CH1 3DY

REQUEST FORM FOR SUNDAY PAPER(S)

SURNAME_____

ROOM NUMBER_____ INITIALS _____

PLEASE ARRANGE FOR THE FOLLOWING SUNDAY NEWSPAPER(S) DATE_____

_____

_____

_____

---

2 Each member of the group is asked to fill in two forms with *different* Sunday newspaper requests on each form.

3 In turn, each group member acts as the receptionist and collects about ten forms. These are put on a database with the room number first and the name of the newspaper(s) next.

4 Calculate how many of each newspaper will be needed from the information on your computer. Enter this information at the foot of your computer records.

CORE SKILL: *Information Technology 1.2 Process information*
PC 1, 2, 3, 4, 5
Range: 1, 2, 3, 4, 5

Situation F – the invoice

1 The room account invoice is put on computer. Put the following hotel details on disk and save them to print out an invoice for each person who filled in a registration form (in Activity 5).

THE HERITAGE HOTEL
Grange Park Lane
Fieldgate
CHESTER
CH1 3DY

Telephone 01454 596387   FAX: 01454 387498

VAT NO 672 1957 62

CUSTOMER'S NAME

Your receptionist

ROOM ACCOUNT INVOICE

Room no	Date	Description	Ref no	Unit Price

NET TOTAL _____

VAT @ 17.5% _____

RECEIVED   TOTAL AMOUNT DUE _____

SIGNED _____

<u>2</u> Recall the room account invoice. Key in the following details, each on a separate invoice, one for each of the registration forms (which you, as the hotel receptionist, were given in Activity 5).

Put your own name against the words 'Your receptionist' and today's date under the column 'Date'.

▶ **Customer 1** (take name, address and room details from form)

DESCRIPTION	REF NO	UNIT PRICE
Bar Sales	19874	3.75
Newspapers	19864	0.58
Corporate	19857	79.00
Restaurant	19836	15.30
Telephone	19859	1.37
	TOTAL	100.00
	VAT	17.50
TOTAL AMOUNT DUE		117.50

▶ **Customer 2** (take name, address and room details from form)

DESCRIPTION	REF NO	UNIT PRICE
Bar Sales	19874	1.25
Restaurant	19836	10.75
Corporate	19857	38.00
	TOTAL	50.00
	VAT	8.75
TOTAL AMOUNT DUE		58.75

▶ **Customer 3** (take name, address and room details from form)

DESCRIPTION	REF NO	UNIT PRICE
Newspapers	19864	0.58
Telephone	19859	1.12
Restaurant	19836	9.30
Corporate	19857	39.00
	TOTAL	50.00
	VAT	8.75
TOTAL AMOUNT DUE		58.75

<u>3</u> Sign each room account after filling in the amount in 'Received'. Keep the forms and the room account invoices for your **Evidence indicator**.

CORE SKILL: *Application of number 1.1 Collect and record data*
Range 1 Technique: obtaining data from written source; obtaining data from people
Communication 1.4 Read and respond to written materials
Range 2, 3, 4
Information Technology 1.1 Prepare information
Range 1, 2, 3, 4, 5
Information Technology 1.1 Present information
Range 1, 2, 3

Case study

Mr Matthews was a visitor who booked in at the Werneth Hotel, Mosstown, for two nights. When he reached his room and switched the television on, he saw this:

Mr Matthews then decided to have a drink at the bar, buy an evening paper and order a meal in the restaurant. He charged these items to his room number. When he returned to the room, the information on the screen had added:

- the price of the room
- the cost of the drink
- the cost of the paper
- the price of the meal.

When he checked out and paid his bill, he knew exactly what the cost would be for his stay at the hotel.

ACTIVITY 8

Write out answers to the following questions in full sentences.

1 Was the greeting in Mr Matthews' room a good idea or not? State reasons for your answer.

2 What was the advantage to the hotel of putting the cost of all the items on computer?

3 Do you think that this was useful for Mr Matthews? Give a reason for your answer.

ACTIVITY 9

Write out the following sentences filling in the missing word(s).

1 Some sales are recorded on an electronic till which prints out details such as the shop _____ and _____.

2 Other tills print a simple receipt showing the cost, the _____ handed over and the _____ given.

3 If customers complain, the organisation is only too pleased to put the matter _____.

4 After 50–60 minutes of continuous keyboard work, the operator should take a _____ minute break.

Situation G – booking coach seats

Work in groups of between 3 and 5 people.

In the following situation, each student in turn plays the part of tour representative who is taking bookings for a coach holiday. The other members of the group play the part of customers. Each customer is the 'lead name' booking seats for one or more people.

1 The tour representative takes bookings from all the customers. Then the next student takes a turn as the tour representative and the others are customers, until everyone has had a turn.

Information for the tour representative

Each person who has booked seats is informed of the price. Adults will pay £10.00 each and children £5.00 each for a seat.

The tour representative keeps a list of the 'lead customer's' name and the total price of the seats. The list will look something like this:

Lead customer's name	Number of adults	Number of children		Total price £
J. Cusik	2	2		30.00
S. Freeman	1			10.00
A. Barnes	1	2		20.00
D. Fielden	2	1		25.00
			TOTAL	85.00

Use the names of your group as lead customers. Total the amount of money for your own list in the same way as it is shown here.

CORE SKILL: *Application of number 1.2 Tackle problems*
Range 1 Technique: Number – working with whole numbers (using addition)
Range 2 Working to a given level of accuracy

2 As the tour representative, take a copy of the following Pick-up Point Sheet and the Booking Sheet for the whole tour (these sheets are to be passed on from one representative to another as each student takes a turn). The last tour representative may find problems in fulfilling customers' requests as the coach fills up!

Each student 'customer' is the lead name for a party of people and may choose the pick-up point for the party. Customers make requests for coach seats; at the front, at the back, together, across the aisle from each other and so on. The tour representative has to try to fulfil the requests and write the names on the booking sheet.

First of all, decide the destination.

Next, decide on three or four places where passengers will be picked up.

PICK-UP POINT SHEET

Day_____ Date_____ Destination_____ Driver's name_____

Pick-up point	Lead customer's name	No. of adults	No. of children

BOOKING SHEET

COLLEGE COACH COMPANY LTD

DESTINATION _____ DATE OF JOURNEY _____

DOOR

DRIVER

1	2
3	4
5	6
7	8
9	10
11	12
13	14
15	16
17	18
19	20
21	22

TOILET AND

SERVING AREA

23	24
25	26
27	28
29	30
31	32
33	34
35	36
37	38	39	40	41

Information stored on the computer which needs to be kept confidential is often accessed only through the use of a password. It is important not to leave details on screen if you are moving away from it. Other confidential details which may be left on the desk for anyone to look at should be put in a locked drawer if you are moving away from it. If you are speaking to customers in front of other people, do not discuss anything which should be private.

Some work may need to be kept confidential.

ACTIVITY 11

Situation H – recording on computer-based systems

Work individually.

A data entry of a standard letter can be made on to the computer which can be altered so that it can be sent to different people giving different details.

1 Put a copy of the following letter on to the computer.

TRANS TRAVEL LTD
29 The Centre
Grange Park
CHESTER   CH2 9JF

Telephone: 0154 398 1176

ABTA NO E1987

FAX: 0154 398 4986

8 December 199–

Miss J. Slater
92 Church Lane
Grange Park
CHESTER   CH9 3KD

Dear Miss Slater

BOOKING REFERENCE 39877675

We give below the details and total cost of your holiday, including the insurance premium agreed at the time of booking:

Tour Operator cost	£700.00
Insurance for one person	£ 50.00
Total amount due	£750.00
Less deposit paid	£100.00
Total balance due	£650.00

In accordance with the usual practice in the holiday industry, we look forward to receiving the balance eight weeks before your holiday begins.

The price has been guaranteed against surcharges and no further invoice will be sent. We would like to take this opportunity of thanking you for your custom and we hope that you will have a delightful holiday.

Your sincerely

Jane Fletcher

Jane Fletcher
BOOKING CLERK

2 As the Booking Clerk, use the standard letter but alter the addressee (the person the letter is sent to) so that it is sent to the following people:

	Mr S. Harrison (PERSON 1) 78 Bamford Road Grange Park CHESTER CH8 3LD	Mr A. Carter (PERSON 2) 187 Main Street Grange Park CHESTER CH8 3OD
Details	**Person 1**	**Person 2**
Tour Operator cost	£650.00	£790.00
Insurance for one person	£50.00	£50.00
Total amount due	£700.00	£840.00
Less deposit paid	£100.00	£100.00
Total balance due	£600.00	£740.00
BOOKING REFERENCE	39877676	39877677

3 Print out one copy of each of the letters. An original copy would be sent to the customer. The copies are to be filed in alphabetical order of the surname and put in a folder.

These copies could be stored in a paper-based system in a filing cabinet. In some systems, the letter would be merged with a database containing the different addresses and costs and could be retrieved from the disk.

CORE SKILL: *Information Technology 1.3 Present information*
Range 1, 2, 3

ACTIVITY 12

1 Write a short paragraph explaining why information technology was being used to send a standard letter to two different people in Activity 11. Mention the advantages of speed, ease of use, and effort and accuracy in using information technology to prepare, process and present the same information, as against using manual methods.

2 Describe the software facilities you used.

CORE SKILL: *Information Technology 1.4 Evaluate the use of information technology*

Health and safety of customers

Health and safety of customers visiting the premises must be considered. A customer may sue the organisation if he or she suffers an injury because of neglect by an employee. For example, fire notices and signs pointing to emergency exits should be in place, and the emergency exit should not be blocked or fastened up in any way so that it could not be used.

Many theme parks aimed at children will suggest a free adult place to a certain number of children. This is so that the children can be adequately supervised and kept safe.

If a party is going by coach, there are rules about the number of hours a driver is allowed to work before stopping for a break. Coach drivers now have to use a tachograph which records the time the coach is moving and the length of any breaks. It also records the speed, so that coaches do not break any limits.

Good housekeeping is a feature in keeping the place safe for customers. The area should be clean and tidy with nothing left lying about for people to fall over.

Any chemicals which may be used (e.g. in swimming pools) should be stored safely and used only by people who know what they are doing. Work equipment should be properly maintained by the employer. Machinery used in a leisure park must be adequately maintained and records kept.

Food hygiene regulations give rules about cleanliness and the correct way to store and prepare food. Any organisation which offers food to customers must comply with these rules and an inspector has the right to check whether the rules are being kept.

People who provide facilities for spectators must make sure that they are reasonably safe for those who use them. A terrifying fire at a football ground, where over a hundred people were injured and fifty-six lost their lives, brought about new rules for spectator sports to make them safe.

ACTIVITY 13

1 Work in a group. Discuss any instances of people being injured or killed while taking part in a leisure or tourism activity that you have heard about. Suggest ways of making the facility safer, or think of new rules which have come into operation because of that particular disaster.

2 One health and safety rule concerns the temperature of a room in which people work. The temperature of the water in a swimming pool and that of the air round it is often of interest to customers. This information is often available in the reception area or on view outside the pool.

Work in a small group of 2 to 4 people. Collect information on either (a) the temperature of the water in your local swimming pool and of the air in the facility, or (b) the temperature of your classroom or base room, for five consecutive days. Make a record of these temperatures and work out the average for each.

CORE SKILL: *Application of number 1.2 Tackle problems*
P.C. 1, 2, 3, 4
Range: Number – working with whole numbers

Employees are obliged to keep any measures which the employer has introduced to meet the terms of the Health and Safety at Work Act. If an employee should wear protective clothing or a helmet, the employer has a right to expect that this will be done. Training in health and safety should be provided, and information about health and safety given out. This could be in a booklet or by notices.

When an employee accepts a job, he or she has agreed not to be careless and to be capable of doing the job. Employees are expected to take care of their own health and safety and that of other people. Keeping to the rules, keeping the place clean and tidy, and taking reasonable care of your own safety and that of others, is a responsibility of those who are employed.

ACTIVITY 14

Write out the following sentences, filling in the missing word(s).

1 Customers may sue an organisation if they are injured because of _____ by an employee.

2 Children should be properly _____ and kept safe.

3 An area visited by customers should be_____ and tidy.

4 Chemicals should be _____ safely.

5 An organisation which provides food must keep the food _____ regulations.

6 Facilities provided for spectators must be _____ for the users.

Problems with completing records

Content

Look back at the records you have completed in this unit. Check through your instructions and make sure that you have done everything which you were asked to do. It is important that all the details are filled in. In the case of an accident, for example, if the correct procedures were not followed and vital information was missed out, the organisation might not be able to prove that there was no neglect.

Legibility

This means writing clearly so that it can be read easily. Take your time and make an effort to write neatly.

Accuracy

When you have completed a record, check through it to make sure that it is accurate. Use the dictionary, the spell-check for written text and check calculations to make sure they are correct.

Format

This usually means filling in a form which may have to be done in a particular way, so that other people can use it for their part of the work. Follow any instructions given to you.

Storing and retrieving records

This can be done manually, in a card index or filing cabinet. Files can be in **subject** order (like *Yellow Pages* where you look under 'B' for 'builder'), or **geographical** order where you look up the location. Both these ways of filing then conform to **alphabetical** order, where filing is in the order of the letters of the alphabet.

Files can also be put on computer and retrieved by using the correct password.

Maintaining the confidentiality of information

Records must be stored in a safe place so that only people with a right to see the information can obtain it. Filing cabinets should be locked, account books kept in the safe, and confidential information on a computer screen should not be left for anyone to see. Don't talk about your work.

Maintaining health and safety

Remember to take breaks from the computer screen, to use proper equipment and furniture, and to take care of your own health and safety and that of other people.

Supervisor

During your work or work experience you will have been introduced to your supervisor. If you have problems with completing records ask for help. In college or school, you will probably ask your tutor. If in doubt, ask! It takes much longer to re-do a piece of work than to find out what is required in the first place.

Colleague with specific skills

Most work is done by teams of people, all of whom have different strengths and weaknesses. The team members will often turn to each other to ask for help where a colleague has a particular skill. In school or college, there are often members of the group with different strengths who will lend a hand if you are struggling.

Colleague with specific responsibilities

This may be the person who is training you. One way of describing training is known as 'Sitting next to Nellie' because the training consisted of the newcomer being told:

'Sit next to Nellie and do what Nellie does.'

This colleague has the responsibility of showing you what to do and if you need help once you start to do the job yourself, you will ask that person.

Refer any problems with maintaining customer records promptly to the appropriate person.

🏃 🏃 🏃 🏃 🏃 **ACTIVITY 15** 🏃 🏃 🏃 🏃 🏃

Write out the following sentences, filling in the missing word(s).

1 To check the content of records, look at your _____ and make sure you have done everything that was required.

2 Legibility is another word for clear and neat _____.

3 Calculations should be _____ to make sure they are correct.

4 It is important to fill in a _____ in a certain way because other people may need to use it for their work.

5 Files in **subject** order can be found in _____ _____.

6 Geographical filing is putting material in the order of the _____.

7 Records should be stored in a safe place so that only people with a _____ to see the information can obtain it.

8 Work may be done by teams of people who have different _____ and weaknesses.

9 A colleague with specific responsibilities who can be approached for help is the person who is _____ you.

10 When in doubt, _____!

Evidence indicator

Your evidence for this element will come from the assessment made by the person observing you dealing with the situations covered.

1 Decide which records you will submit for:

   ▶ storing and retrieving records correctly and securely
   ▶ maintaining the confidentiality of information stored on customer records
   ▶ ensuring health and safety when using recording systems
   ▶ referring any problems with maintaining records promptly to the appropriate person.

2 You should also check that your customer records are completed legibly, accurately and in the correct format.

3 Write up your evaluation of your evidence, judging the work you have done against the activity you were asked to perform. Mention any difficulties or problems you had when dealing with your 'customers'.

4 If you have been able to use work experience, work shadowing or your own observation of maintaining customer records, write a short account of this and add it to your evidence.

Evaluation

Look at the activities you have undertaken for this unit.

1 Check the work you have done against the activities to see that you have answered all the questions and completed all the work.

2 Look at the other ways you could have used to do the activities (for example, writing instead of word processing) and say why you chose your particular way to do the work.

3 Now you have finished, have you any ideas for improving your work in future?

   Write out a short statement about this, heading it 'Evaluation'.

Revision and specimen test questions

Focus 4: Maintaining customer records

Reference: Element 1.3 PC1, PC3, PC4, PC5

External test requirements

a *Recognise how to complete different customer records accurately and in the correct format, from given data.*

Range

Customer records: customer information (personal details, financial details), customer sales, customer enquiries and customer complaints

Customer information may be kept in a manual filing system or on computer. The details are usually the customer's name, address, telephone number and any necessary financial details. Customer sales are recorded on a receipt, either handwritten or produced on an electronic till, carrying details of the person who sold the goods, the money received and the date. Customer enquiries may turn into orders so records should show name, address and telephone number of the customer and details of what was wanted.

1 Copy and complete the following Customer Enquiry Form using the details which follow.

ENQUIRY

GRANGE PARK RESTAURANT
Fieldgate
CHESTER

FUNCTION _____

NAME OF CUSTOMER _____

ADDRESS _____

TELEPHONE NUMBER _____

DATE_____ TIME _____

APPROXIMATE PRICE PER HEAD _____

OTHER DETAILS _____

_____

Details
Function: Annual Office Christmas Party
Name of customer: J. W. Barnes & Co Ltd
Address: 49 High Street, Fieldgate, Chester
CH2 8TR
Telephone number: 0131 348287
Date: 13 December (this year)

Time: 1930 hours
Other details: Price required for a buffet
supper for about 23 people.
Private room required.

2 Copy and fill in the following handwritten
receipt using the details which follow.

HERITAGE HOUSE CRAFT SHOP
Grange Park
CHESTER   CH3 9TR

Received from..

the sum of ....

for ....

Date...

SIGNED ....

Details
Received from: J. Benson
the sum of £32.00
for eight tins of Lakeland Fudge
Date: (today)
Signed: C. Shawcross (Miss)

3 Copy and fill out the following Customer
Complaint Form using the details which
follow.

GRANGE PARK LEISURELAND
COMPLAINT FORM

NAME OF COMPLAINANT _____

ADDRESS _____

TELEPHONE NUMBER _____

DATE OF INCIDENT OR COMPLAINT _____

DETAILS OF COMPLAINT

DETAILS TAKEN BY _____ DATE _____

SIGNED (MEMBER OF STAFF) _____

SIGNED (COMPLAINANT) _____

Details
Name: Balkees Zaman
Address: 14 Church Lane, Fieldgate, Chester
CH9 3KL
Telephone: 0131 597296
Date of incident: (yesterday's date)
Details:

The complainant stated that when she
entered the reception area of the college in
the morning, she slipped and fell. The floor
was inspected and it was found that oil had
been spilled. There was oil on the sole of
Miss Zaman's shoe. She claimed that the oil
was a hazard and had caused her to fall.

Taken by: Morris Stephenson
Complainant: Balkees Zaman

External test requirements

b *Recognise how to maintain
confidentiality of information stored on
computer records.*

Range

Confidentiality of information in relation to
customer information (personal details,
financial details), customer complaints,
customer enquiries, customer requests, sales

Confidentiality of information must be
maintained and only those entitled to know
should see records. Information on
computer should be accessed only through
a password. Information should not be left
on screen or on paper for anyone to see.
Confidential files should be locked away.

Private information should not be discussed with other people.

4 A business person staying at a hotel requests the receptionist to state how much the firm is paying for the hotel room. The receptionist should:
   a bring up the invoice on computer and give details
   b ask the porter if he knows the business person
   c state that she cannot give that information
   d offer to send a copy of the invoice to the person's home

External test requirements

c *Recognise how to ensure health and safety when using recording systems.*

Range

Health and safety of customers, of self, of colleagues

Regular display screen-workers who use the screen for more than three hours a day, should not use screen-based systems for more than an hour at a time without a break. Employers should provide free eye-tests and, if necessary, spectacles. Work-stations should be comfortable. Workers should use the correct posture, both at the display screen and when writing.

5 A full-time library assistant uses the computer to bring up details of customers and their books when checking out further books. As a health and safety measure, she is entitled to:
   a free eye tests
   b a break from library duties every hour
   c lounge on the chair in front of the screen
   d use the computer to book holidays

External test requirements

d *Recognise problems with maintaining customer records, and identify the appropriate person to report given problems to.*

Range

Problems with completing records (content, legibility, accuracy, format), with storing and retrieving records, with maintaining the confidentiality of information, with maintaining health and safety. Appropriate persons: supervisor, colleague with specific skills, colleague with specific responsibilities

Records must be completed accurately. If they are written, the writing must be legible. Filing must be done carefully so that records can be retrieved. Confidential information should be locked in a filing cabinet, account books should be kept in the safe and passwords should be used to access private information held on computer.

In cases of difficulty, supervisors or more experienced colleagues should be consulted.

6 A work experience student in a travel agency adds some customer information to a database which records the customers who require to be met at the airport by the agency's own transport. He is not sure how to print out the information. Which person should he approach for help?
   a the driver of the transport
   b the experienced travel agency clerk
   c his own tutor from college
   d the customer whose details have just been recorded

Preparing visitor information materials

element 2.1

Describe major visitor attractions in the UK

Recreation

Entertainment, exercise, pastimes and sport are all part of the recreation industry. Examples of recreational attractions include national parks and tourist attractions. If your *Yellow Pages* has a section called 'The Inside Guide', it will give details of country parks in your area which are attractive to people looking for recreation because they offer acres of park and woodland to walk in, nature trails, lakes with watersports, fishing and watching wildlife. Moorland, rivers and streams, scenic walks, splendid views and more formal gardens, form a wealth of recreational opportunities.

All kinds of sporting activities are found nationally, from the football stadiums and cricket pitches, to the National Cycling Velodrome where spectators as well as people taking part can enjoy the sport.

You can also find details of art galleries, museums, exhibitions, parks and gardens in *Yellow Pages* and in your local *Thomson* directory. Travel agents and coach tour operators will also have details of attractions and organised trips which visit them. More information can be obtained from your local Tourist Information Centre.

Tourists can be anyone from the day visitor, people staying with friends or relatives to see something of their area, to visitors from abroad spending time in the UK. Besides recreational facilities, they will probably be interested in the history of the region, the National Trust houses and stately homes which have wonderful collections of furniture, original portraits, needlework, silver, tapestry and elaborate painted ceilings to view.

Culture and entertainment

Many tourist attractions contain heritage sites and industrial museums which specialise in various commercial developments. Quite a few will allow hands on experience with working machinery to operate, which older children particularly enjoy.

There are craft centres, art galleries and museums with interesting features to be found in large cities, and time can be spent, whatever the weather, in a rich centre of historical interest.

Entertainment details may also be found in 'The Inside Guide' in *Yellow Pages* or under the subject headings of: Cinemas, Discos and Dance Halls, Night Clubs, Entertainers, Public Houses, Restaurants, Theatres and Concert Halls. There are dance venues and concert halls for classical, jazz and rock music to suit many different tastes.

Children's attractions

The local Tourist Information Centre will have a wealth of information about attractions for children. Look under: Fun Parks, Theme Parks, Farms and Zoos, Canal Cruises and Local Attractions in *Yellow Pages* for some ideas. Many of these attractions are suitable for a day out with children, either with the family, or perhaps in a school class outing.

The Runaway Mine Train at Alton Towers.

 **ACTIVITY 1**

To identify the main tourist attractions it is useful to have up-to-date information. The British Tourist Authority address is:

Thames Tower
Black's Road
LONDON
W6 9EL

They publish a leaflet on *National Facts of Tourism* (price 50p). Decide how many copies of this your group will need and write a letter asking for copies. Your letter may be put on the word processor and a copy printed for everyone who is in the group. You may give your college address, but be sure to add the name of your tutor and your department, as the office staff may not know who you are and a reply could go astray! Alternatively, you could give your own address. Put the correct year instead of the dots.

Example of letter

British Tourist Authority
Thames Tower
Black's Road
LONDON
W6 9EL

Mosstown College of Further Education
Ashley Road
MOSSTOWN
M9 1GJ

8 January . . . . .
Dear Sirs

I am a student at the above College on a Leisure and Tourism Course. I should be glad if you would let me have three copies of the latest NATIONAL FACTS OF TOURISM leaflet and I enclose a postal order for £1.50 in payment.

Please address the leaflets for the attention of my tutor, Ms Jane Arnold, Leisure and Tourism Department. We look forward to receiving this information.

Yours faithfully

Catherine Ryan

Catherine Ryan

Once you have completed the letter send it off; the leaflet will be useful for the next activity where you will be doing some research on the visitor attractions available in your own area. If you think about the possibility of entertaining a friend or relative for three or four days in your own area, where would you take them each day? The group may have plenty of ideas but there could be attractions which you haven't thought about.

ACTIVITY 2

Work with a group of 2 to 4 people.

1 Look through directories (such as *Thomson* and *Yellow Pages*) and back copies of newspapers (your college library will probably have these) for advertisements about recreation in your area. Visit your local tourist information centre and your travel agent. Collect information, leaflets, advertisements and posters about major visitor attractions.

2 Sort out your information under the following headings:

▶ recreation
▶ culture and entertainment
▶ children's attractions.

3 Put all the visitor attractions under each heading in alphabetical order.

4 Take one or two headings each. Make a list which states:

▶ the name of the attraction
▶ the address
▶ the telephone number.

Save the information. Print out a copy for yourself and one for each member of the group.

5 Go through your attractions again. Make sure that at least two attractions use natural resources, e.g. a water park, a national park or beautiful scenery. Alter your information if necessary and print out a revised copy. Attach this to the original copy.

6 Make up a questionnaire to find out which attractions are considered best by:

▶ families
▶ teenagers
▶ adults not going with children.

Each person in the group should ask at least five people – family, friends, other students in the college, tutors, support staff (if they have time to answer!).

7 Make a bar chart of the results of the questionnaire to show which attractions three kinds of people who were questioned preferred most.

CORE SKILL: *Information Technology 1.1 Prepare information*
PC 1, 2, 3, 4
Range 2 (Information graphics), 4 (Software graphics)

Case study

'Eureka!' is a word which we all associate with discovery and it is also the name of the award-winning museum for children at Halifax. Among the awards it has won are the English Tourist Board's 'Visitor attraction of the year' and Tommy's Campaign 'Most parent friendly museum'.

In this museum everyone can touch, listen and smell as well as look. If children like the hands on approach, this is the place for it. Children enjoy trying out the Music Box which is full of musical inventions they can touch to make unusual sounds.

Role-playing an adult's working life, finding out how bodies work, sending hi-tech messages and finding out how water, gas and electricity come into the home are only some of the things to discover as visitors pass through the three exhibition areas and use the exhibits.

The museum has been especially designed for children up to the age of 12 but can be enjoyed by all visitors, including those with disabilities and special needs.

There is recorded information about opening times and admission prices on telephone number 0142 6983191 which is available 24 hours a day. There are special prices for groups and the museum can be reached by road (there is a car park) or by rail as Eureka! is situated next to the railway station.

ACTIVITY 3

Answer the following questions in full sentences.

1 Where is the museum situated?

2 State one of the awards which the museum has won.

3 What is different about this museum and the ones where exhibits are put into cases and labelled?

4 How many exhibition areas are there in this museum?

5 If you wished to take a group, how would you find out details of cost and opening hours?

Work individually.

You discover that the admission price for a group to the Eureka! museum is £3.00 per child, minimum ten children. One adult is admitted free with every ten children. Extra adults would be charged £5.00 each.

Mosstown Junior School ask you to work out a price for their Year 6 class. They will visit the museum with the class teacher, the school secretary and a mother who has volunteered to be a helper for the day. There are 31 children in the class. What would it cost?

CORE SKILL: *Application of number 1.1 Collect and record data*
PC 1, 2, 3, 4
Range 1 (Handling data) 3 (Units of money)

What attracts the visitors?

Many tourist attractions are in their present location because of natural features or resources. Seaside holiday resorts are obvious examples, with sandy beaches, the sea, surrounded by beautiful countryside. This makes them very popular with visitors. Holiday centres make use of rivers for canoeing, the countryside for pony trekking, hills and moorland for walking holidays.

Heritage museums, historic houses and stately homes may now have a substitute for the tour guide. Tourists wear a walkman which gives them recorded information as they walk around the attraction. This may be provided in different languages. Some attractions have guides who can speak to visitors in their own language.

Most attractions have facilities, such as access for wheelchair users, first-aid posts and places to change babies' nappies. Tourists may also need accommodation, food, toilet facilities, information leaflets and books and souvenirs to take away. Most attractions have information leaflets giving details of parking, 'lost children post', whether it is suitable for dogs on leads or disabled people and the cost, and include a telephone number. At the end of the tour, there is usually a shop where craft goods or souvenirs may be bought.

The beautiful countryside of the Lake District in Cumbria.

ACTIVITY 5

_1_ Use the database of local attractions which you made for Activity 2. Choose two attractions that you can find more information for, e.g. you may be able to obtain leaflets or advertisements about them.

_2_ Word process a short account of each of your two attractions, and mention:

- the main features of the attraction
- any products or services which it offers
- anything which is special or unusual about the attraction

Save this first version of your account.

_3_ Spell-check your work and correct any typing errors. Ask your tutor to check for any further errors.

Correct the draft with your tutor observing you and then print out a corrected second draft.

_4_ Ask your tutor to sign both the first and second drafts to say that you have been observed making corrections and saving your work.

CORE SKILL: _Information Technology 1.1 Prepare information_
_PC 1, 2, 3, 4_
Range 1, 2, 3, 4, 5

Location

Natural features are one reason for the location of visitor attractions. There may be plenty of space to expand into, for a theme park or a zoo. A building may be available for converting into a heritage centre. The visitor could experience going down a coal mine or watch actors in period costume recreating history in an industrial setting. Many industries offer tours of their premises. Power stations, breweries, chocolate factories and potteries all show the visitor how it is done and their location ties in with the area's natural features. Potteries grew up near the clay they need; nuclear power stations are situated away from residential areas.

There is no point in having an attraction for visitors, if it is so far from where people live that there are no staff to run it or people to visit it. The top 20 attractions in the country are near to population centres and transport routes. For day visitors, a journey of up to two hours each way leaves enough time to enjoy the attraction, so those which are in the centre of the country will be able to draw on large numbers of day visitors. If they are near motorways, those who wish to visit can come from considerable distances.

Attractions in large towns will have tourists who can use coaches, buses and trains, as well as cars, so more people are able to visit them.

Work individually.

1 Look at your *National Facts of Tourism* leaflet which you sent for in Activity 1. Choose one or two attractions from this list which are nearest to the area you live in. If you make only one choice, look at your own list of local attractions and pick one of those for your second choice.

2 Work in pairs.

   Discuss the two attractions you have chosen with your partner. Decide why they are in their present location. Are they:

   ◗ in the centre of the country so that many people can travel there?

   ◗ near to other tourist attractions?

   ◗ in a tourist resort or centre?

   ◗ easy to get to by public transport or private transport?

   ◗ using natural features (e.g. a lake, the seaside)?

   ◗ a part of the history of the place?

   ◗ or are there any other reasons you can think of?

3 When you have your information and ideas ready, ask your tutor to observe your discussion.

4 Word process or write out a short account of your discussion, setting out the views of both partners. Ask your tutor to sign this account as an assessor of your **Core skill** *Communication 1.1 PC1, PC2, PC3, PC4.*

ACTIVITY 7

1 Choose one of the attractions from Activity 6 and find its position on a map of the United Kingdom.

2 Sketch or copy the map showing the position of the attraction in relation to the nearest motorways, rail stations or other transport routes.

3 Mark on the map the position of two nearby population centres and label them.

CORE SKILL: *Communication 1.3 Use images PC 1, 2, 3 Range 1, 2, 3 – image used to illustrate a point*

ACTIVITY 8

Write out the following sentences, filling in the missing word(s).

1 Entertainment, exercise, pastimes and _____ are all part of the recreation industry.

2 Tourists can be day visitors or tourists from _____.

3 Culture includes craft centres, art galleries and _____.

4 Entertainment can cover concert halls, cinemas and _____.

5 Children's attractions include fun parks and _____ parks.

6 Local attractions can be found in directories such as _____ _____.

Case study

Many pubs are now making efforts to attract families for meals. Sunday lunch is offered from midday until the evening and there are special menus for children.

Youngsters are often offered crayons and a picture to fill in, to occupy them until the meal is ready. Many pubs have a special room filled with ballpools, climbing frames, bouncy plastic hills, slides and sandpits, both inside and outside. The best equipped places are an attraction both for local people and those travelling some distance. From being a place where children were once unwelcome, the pub with its garden full of activity play equipment is now a place where children can enjoy an outing with family and friends.

ACTIVITY 9

Answer the following questions in full sentences.

1 What is the advantage of a pub which offers facilities for families?

2 What is the attraction to parents of a pub with play equipment?

3 What other suggestions can you think of to make a pub more attractive to families?

4 Have you seen the trend to attract families in any other tourist activity (such as shopping) by providing facilities? If so, describe what you have seen.

The needs of different visitors

Tourists have certain primary needs. They must have:

▸ **attractions and amenities** which may be anything from theatres to sports centres, national parks, heritage centres, theme parks, beauty spots, museums or industrial centres
▸ **information** which may be obtained from guidebooks and brochures before they arrive, from reception desks in hotels, from Tourist Information Centres, libraries, maps, tourist guides, leaflets and signposts
▸ **accommodation** which varies with the amount of money they wish to spend and could be a hotel, guesthouse, motel, bed-and-breakfast, self-catering, caravan, tent on camping site, university campus (when students are away) or staying with relatives or friends

▶ **catering** which may be available as part of their package holiday, or they may eat in a restaurant, café or pub, or have fast food, snacks or takeaway food.

Needs related to age

Children have special needs. Many attractions offer baby-changing facilities, group bookings for school parties, first-aid and lost children posts. Toilet facilities are essential, picnic areas are useful. There should be enough room for people with pushchairs to allow others to pass. Some theme parks have a height restriction on certain rides to help to ensure the safety of children – this saves arguments about whether a child is old enough or not to go on the ride!

Elderly visitors appreciate lifts as well as stairs, and need plenty of time to look at exhibitions or historical and heritage centres, and somewhere to sit down at the end of it all. Wheelchair users and other people with mobility difficulties appreciate ramps and lifts; disabled toilets are also necessary.

If there are people with hearing difficulties listening to the guide, he or she should face them so that facial expression and perhaps lip-reading helps them to understand. Speaking slowly (but not shouting) also helps. Partially-sighted people will be guided by a voice and it is best to touch them gently to draw their attention to any hazards. They may need to take an arm to move around and it is helpful to mention any steps to go up or down. Guide dogs are allowed in catering establishments even when other dogs are forbidden.

Foreign visitors may also need help. It is hard to understand another language if it is spoken quickly, so slow down and pronounce words properly. Check if you have been understood. Gestures and facial expressions also help in communicating. Educational materials for students may be available in various languages and the tour guide (or the walkman recording), may be in different languages.

Baby changing

First Aid

Parking

Access for wheelchair users

Telephone

Dogs on leads

 **ACTIVITY 10**

Send off for (or collect from your local tourist information centre, library or other source) leaflets about major visitor attractions. Read them carefully, and then make a list of the ways in which they meet the special needs of visitors (i.e. parking for the disabled, facilities for children).

Types of visitors

Main tourist attractions and resorts (e.g. London) often have many different types of visitors who all find something to enjoy. Adults may be interested in entertainment or in sport, enjoy an insight into history or want to glimpse the world of science. They may want to look at beautiful scenery or enjoy looking at wildlife.

Families may also enjoy the fun of a large theme park or be fascinated by the strange creatures in a zoo or nature reserve. Museums may specialise in collections in one particular field; children's theatre can provide a special treat. 'Finding out' is popular; youngsters like to see how TV programmes are produced and walk through the sets which are seen on the small screen.

UK residents staying overnight are the largest group of tourists in the UK, followed by UK residents on day trips, who are almost matched by overseas visitors coming to the UK. Day visitors may go to places in their own area or they may go to another part of the country for the day.

The industrial heritage of the UK provides enjoyment for UK and overseas visitors alike. Famous cities are popular with visitors, e.g. Stratford-upon-Avon with its Shakespearean connection, Edinburgh at the time of its famous festival, or London with its museums and historical sights. Manchester was high on the list of visitor attractions in 1995, with its new sports arenas, Nynex Leisure Complex and Concert Hall, shops, theatres and many other attractions within easy reach.

ACTIVITY 11

Work in pairs.

Look at the *National Facts of Tourism* leaflet published by the British Tourist Authority.

1. From the table 'Distribution of tourism' pick out:
   a where the largest number of UK residents went last year
   b where the largest number of overseas visitors went last year.

2. Look at the table 'Countries of origin' and pick out:

   a where most of the overseas visitors came from
   b which two European countries sent the most overseas visitors to the UK.

3. Look on the front cover of your *National Facts of Tourism* leaflet to find out the area where most overseas visitors went last year.

   Choose a town or city in that area.

4. Write or word process a letter to the tourist information centre, town hall (add

the town or city you have chosen) and state that you have noticed that most overseas visitors come from (give the names of the two countries of origin in Europe you have picked out) and suggest that leaflets for main attractions should also be printed in these two languages.

<u>5</u> Print or write out an original copy. Check your letter for spelling (use the spell-check on the word processor) and then ask your tutor to check that version. Make any necessary corrections and make another copy. Ask your tutor to verify that you have been observed making corrections to your letter.

CORE SKILL: *Information Technology 1.1*
PC 1, 2, 3, 4.

 **ACTIVITY 12**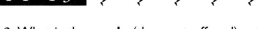

A theme park attracts the following number of visitors in the months shown.

Use Information Technology to show this by means of bar charts.

CORE SKILL: *Information Technology 1.3 Present*
information
PC 1, 2, 3, 4
Range 1 (graphics) 2, 3 (graphics)

Month	Number of visitors (thousands)
January	9
February	9
March	10
April	12
May	13
June	13
July	15
August	15
September	12
October	11
November	9
December	9

 **ACTIVITY 13**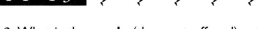

You apply for a job as a counter assistant in a snack bar in your local ice skating rink. The following rates of pay are listed.

Day	per hour (£)
Sunday	5.00
Monday	2.50
Tuesday	2.50
Wednesday	2.50
Thursday	2.50
Friday	3.00
Saturday	3.00

Answer the following in full sentences.

<u>1</u> What is the **mean** (the average) rate of pay per hour?

<u>2</u> What is the **mode** (the most offered) rate of pay per hour?

<u>3</u> If you worked for three hours each day for seven days a week, what would you earn?

<u>4</u> If you could only work for two days each week, which days would you choose and why?

CORE SKILL: *Application of number 1.3 Interpret*
and present data
PC 2, 4
Range: 2 (Techniques) Number –
interpreting mode and mean

Transport links

Most tourists in the UK travel by car and this is seen as the most convenient way to travel from door to door. Coach travel is another very popular way to travel for business and holiday visitors. Some coach services provide refreshments for travellers. Day tours and holidays are popular with many people.

Coaches, cars and buses may cause congestion and pollution in cities and some places introduce 'park and ride' schemes for cars. A coach is one of the least expensive ways to travel for long distances.

Rail travel has declined in popularity with tourists, though holiday-makers can take advantage of cheaper fares if they do not travel at peak periods. Special excursions by steam locomotives have proved to be an attraction, especially at Christmas time when Santa travels on various Santa Claus special trains and gives out presents to the children on board!

Overseas travellers who wish to use their cars when they come to the UK can come by ferry. Visitors can also use the hovercraft for a quick journey across the channel.

The opening of the Channel Tunnel has meant that tourists from Europe can be in the UK in 35 minutes. Lorries, cars and coaches are loaded on to Le Shuttle. Passengers use the Eurostar train service which takes three hours to get to Paris from London. There are also night sleepers for more distant journeys.

Air travel is one of the most popular ways to travel to the UK from other parts of the world. Most visitors go to London. Manchester Airport has the most traffic outside South East England and is currently waiting for a decision on a second runway. In 1995, visitors from America to Manchester were a record number.

Tourists travel by road, sea, air and rail.

🏃 🏃 🏃 🏃 🏃 **ACTIVITY 14** 🏃 🏃 🏃 🏃 🏃

Work in pairs.

Choose a tourist attraction in the centre of your nearest town. Write down as many different types of transport as possible which might be used to bring visitors to the attraction from your own area and from other parts of the UK.

Cost of visits

Many attractions have special concessions for school parties, family groups or people on a pension. Individual visitors usually pay the full rate. Sometimes customers can get cut-price rates when it becomes obvious that the seats on a plane are not going to be taken up at full price. It is better to obtain a price which does not give a profit than to make a loss on the seat. Costs of visits have to be calculated so that the visitor thinks the price fair and the organisation can make a profit.

ACTIVITY 15

Write out the following sentences, filling in the missing word(s).

1 Most tourists in the UK travel by _____.

2 _____ travel has declined in popularity with tourists.

3 Visitors can use the _____ for quick journeys across the channel.

4 Visitors from overseas can travel the whole way by rail if they use the _____ _____.

5 _____ travel is one of the most popular ways for people to travel to the UK from other parts of the world.

6 Most visitors who travelled to the UK by air went to _____.

Evidence indicator

1 Discuss examples of the three main types of visitor attractions listed below (see Activity 2):

   ▶ recreation
   ▶ culture and entertainment
   ▶ children's attractions.

   Choose one attraction from each category for the group to visit.

2 Make arrangements for a group visit to each of the chosen visitor attractions. Before the visit is made, word process the following headings. Fill in the information either before, during or after the visit (as you decide which is the most appropriate way).

- The main features of the attraction and its main products and services
- The location of the attraction (is it within a two-hour drive of areas where people live?)
- Transport links to the attraction
- The different types of visitors and their requirements
- The appeal of the attraction to different visitor types (old, young, adults, groups?)
- The cost of a visit to this attraction for:
  - individuals
  - family groups
  - people entitled to special concessions (are there any extra costs?).

3 From your database, give two more examples of major visitor attractions taken from:

- recreation
- culture and entertainment
- children's attractions.

State what their main features, products and services are. The information may be taken from brochures, leaflets, guidebooks, maps or other sources.

Evaluation

Go through your activities. Write a short account of:

- ideas which were good
- ideas which didn't work – with the reason why if you know it
- any improvements which you think could have been made
- whether your information was correct
- what you did to check to make sure everything had been done.

Revision and specimen test questions

Focus 1: Major visitor attractions

Reference: Element 2.1 PC1, PC2

External test requirements

a *Recognise descriptions of the types of major visitor attractions in the UK, and identify examples of each type.*

Range

Types of major visitor attractions: recreation, culture and entertainment, children's attractions

Recreation includes exercise, pastimes and sport. Cultural entertainment includes libraries, museums and art galleries, historical and heritage sites, theatres, cinemas and concert halls. Children's attractions are fun parks, zoos, playgrounds, working farms and theme parks.

1 An example of a major visitor attraction for children would be:
   a Suncars Leisure Car Hire
   b Mini cruises from Harwich to Holland
   c Pleasure Island Theme Park
   d Robinson's coach holidays

2 Tourists looking for a cultural experience would be most likely to visit:
   a Aqua Park, Norfolk
   b The Wildlife Tropical House
   c Eurotunnel Exhibition Centre
   d Egyptian section of Manchester Museum

3 Recreational and sporting activities for visitors can be found at:
   a Suffolk Wildlife Park
   b Grasscroft Leisure Centre
   c Bressingham Steam Museum and Gardens
   d Martinmere Bird Sanctuary

External test requirements

b *Recognise the main features, products and services of given major attractions in the UK.*

Range

Features, products and services; natural features, built features: size, variety of attractions, additional services, family facilities

Features may be natural features, e.g. hills, mountains, water. Features which have been built include, e.g. a climbing wall in a sports hall. The size of the attraction is also a feature, e.g. a large theme park (such as Alton Towers in Staffordshire). Theme parks have a variety of attractions and additional services, such as food, toilet facilities, parking and first-aid.

4 Which of the following services offered by Colchester Zoo would make it particularly suitable for children to visit?
   a returning endangered species to the wild
   b restaurant with terrace for meals
   c free car parking
   d birthday outing with cake and goody bags

5 Which two of the following are examples of a manufactured product attracting visits from tourists?
   1 Caithness Crystal Visitor Centre
   2 Tropical Leisure Pool
   3 Great Yarmouth Pleasure Beach
   4 The Potteries China Experience

   Choose from:
   a 1 and 2
   b 2 and 3
   c 3 and 4
   d 1 and 4

6 Which of the following attractions relies on a natural feature to interest visitors?
   a White Knuckle Ride at Blackpool Pleasure Beach
   b The Craft and Skills Village
   c Snape Maltings river trips
   d The Gallery of English Costume, Manchester

Focus 2: Location and transport links

Reference: Element 2.1 PC3, PC6

External test requirements

a *Recognise the location of given major UK visitor attractions.*

Range

Location: in relation to population centres, in relation to major transport routes, in relation to position on the UK map

The location of an attraction is an important factor for visitors. It must be near to, or easily reached from, major population centres. Visitors arrive by major transport routes in cars, coaches, buses and by rail. Those attractions which are in the centre of the country can draw their visitors from anywhere within reasonable travelling distance. London also attracts many visitors from abroad, who can now use Eurotunnel as well as aeroplanes.

7 Blackpool Pleasure Beach is located where:
   a people find it hard to travel to
   b there are many population centres nearby
   c accommodation is very limited
   d there are no other attractions

8 Which two of the following reasons make London's visitor attractions easy to attend?
   1 they are open 24 hours a day
   2 there is a lost children post for day visitors
   3 there are road and rail links from all over the UK
   4 many overseas visitors can arrive by air

   Choose from:
   a 1 and 2
   b 2 and 3
   c 3 and 4
   d 1 and 4

External test requirements

b *Identify the transport links taking visitors to given major UK visitor attractions.*

Range

Transport links: air, rail, road, ferry

Transport links taking people to visitor attractions in the UK are mainly by road: coaches, cars and buses. Many places can be reached by rail and some places can be reached by sea. Major cities have airports so that visitors from abroad can reach centres easily.

9 Which of the following transport links would be most likely to be used by a tour operator taking American visitors round the stately homes of the UK?
   a private railway carriage
   b aeroplanes
   c ferries
   d coach

Focus 3: Visitor types

Reference: Element 2.1 PC4, PC5

External test requirements

a *Identify the needs of different types of visitor using given attractions.*

Range

Needs: related to age, related to the purpose of the visit, related to any specific requirements; needs for additional services

Visitor needs related to age include children who need first-aid facilities, lost children posts, toilets and snack bars. Elderly visitors may need lifts and somewhere to sit down. Visitors may need information about the attraction and its facilities. Special requirements include toilets, ramps and lifts for wheelchair users and removing anything which may prove a hazard for partially-sighted people. Foreign tourists may need pictures or diagrams to help them understand instructions (such as Fire Exit).

Types of visitors may be adults, families, UK-based and from outside the UK.

10 Which two of the following would a party of school children visiting a theme park be most likely to need?
   1 first-class restaurant for lunch

2 first-aid post
3 lost children facility
4 map from the school to the theme park

Choose from:
a 1 and 2
b 2 and 3
c 3 and 4
d 1 and 4

11 Tourists from outside the UK visiting an attraction would be most likely to need:
   a signs with pictures or diagrams to show facilities
   b a tour guide who speaks only English
   c passports to show before they enter an attraction
   d letter boxes to post letters home

External test requirements

b *Recognise the appeal of given visitor attractions to different types of visitor.*

Range

Appeal of selected visitor attractions: history, landscape, entertainment, cost, ease of access, recreation, specific interests

Visitors will each have different views about what makes an attraction appealing. They may enjoy history, admire the landscape or be looking for entertainment. Cost is always a factor and visitors must be able to travel to the attraction. They may enjoy recreation pursuits, such as walking, climbing and sports. They may have specific interests (e.g. following a football team).

12 Which of the following visitor types would be most likely to visit a safari park?
   a football team supporters
   b families with children
   c golfing enthusiasts
   d swimming club members

13 A theatre performance of the musical 'My Fair Lady' would be most likely to attract an audience of:

a small children

b families from abroad

c adults

d teenagers

Investigate local visitor information materials

Types of visitor

People travel away from their homes for business, personal reasons or for pleasure. Anyone who travels away from home for whatever reason, not just to be on holiday, is classed as a tourist. Business travellers account for about a third of the tourist market. Besides British people taking holidays, there were 19.5 million tourists visiting Britain in 1993. Most of these (12.5 million) came from Western Europe, 3.4 million from North America and 3.6 million from the rest of the world. Visitors from the Far East are now a fast-growing group.

To classify tourists into local and national, it is useful to think of local tourists as day visitors. National tourists are those who visit other localities within the UK but stay overnight. International visitors only form a small part of the tourist industry but they spend a relatively large amount of money in proportion to their number, as they usually stay in hotel accommodation and buy souvenirs to take home.

Tourists going out of, or coming into, this country usually book their holiday as a package through a travel agent which provides them with their accommodation and catering needs, but they still need information about attractions and places of interest to see in the UK.

Visitors to the local area are adults and families, and these can be based in the UK or from outside the UK. They may already have a programme of things to do and places to see, or they may be looking for interesting things to do which they decide on after arrival.

There are two ways of researching the information which you will need for these visitors. One is called 'desk research' where you sit at your desk and look things up in books, brochures,

Types of visitors include families.

TO: All concerned with GNVQ (see circulation list)

FROM: Mary Moore, GNVQ Co-ordinator

DATE: 13.10.99

SUBJECT: GNVQ TUTOR SUPPORT GROUP MEETING

The next GNVQ Tutor Support Group Meeting will take place at 3.15 p.m. on Wednesday 16th February in Room C23, Redditch Campus. One theme of the meeting will be to up-date tutors on Curriculum 2000 and GNVQ, but if you have other agenda items that you wish to raise please will you let me know as soon as possible (see below).

New members of staff and staff who will be tackling GNVQ for the first time in September are especially welcome. This forum gives the opportunity to discuss issues of common interest or concern, and can generate ideas and suggestions relating to the GNVQ programme within the college. Many colleagues have in the past benefited from this sharing of experience and ideas.

newspapers and magazines; and the other way is to visit places yourself, ask questions, observe and write down what you see.

Local directories (such as *Yellow Pages* and *Thomson*) have information about tourist attractions in your own area on certain pages. *Yellow Pages* or the Phone Book will also give you the address and telephone number of various centres which will help with information. Look under:

▶ Tourist Information Centres
▶ Tourist Information Services
▶ Travel Agents and Tour Operators
▶ Visitor Information Centre
▶ Leisure Services
▶ Libraries
▶ Information Services.

You will need to use both research methods in order to find out what you need to know.

ACTIVITY 1

Write out the following sentences, filling in the missing word(s).

1 People travel away from their homes for _____ or personal reasons.

2 Anyone who travels away from home is classed as a _____.

3 Local tourists are often thought of as being _____ visitors.

4 International tourists form only a small part of the industry but they spend a relatively _____ amount of money in proportion to their number.

5 Most foreign tourists to the UK come from _____ _____.

6 Visitors from the _____ _____ are a fast-growing group.

ACTIVITY 2

Look at the leaflet you obtained from the British Tourist Authority and find the table 'Distribution of tourism'.

1 Use your own region for information and answer the following questions in full sentences.
   a How many trips were made by UK residents?
   b How much did they spend?
   c How many trips were made by visitors from overseas?
   d How much did they spend?
   e Where did most of the visitors come from?
   f What was the total income to your region from visitors?

2 Look at the table 'Purpose of tourism' on

the same leaflet. Answer the following questions in full sentences.

a What was the main purpose of trips undertaken by UK residents?

b What was the main purpose of trips undertaken by overseas visitors?

c What was the second most frequent reason given for trips by overseas visitors?

d How much was spent altogether by tourists last year? (Answer in millions.)

Common information needs

When visitors come to stay on holiday in an area, or when they are taking a day's outing from home, they need to know the location of the place they propose to visit.

Leaflets from the Tourist Information Centre often have maps showing the nearest motorway, because about 86% of their visitors will use road transport. On the motorway itself, and on the roads leading to the attraction, there will be signs indicating the direction to take. This kind of information is useful both to UK residents and visitors from overseas, because signs are easy to read and follow.

The next need is to know when the attraction is open, so that journeys are not undertaken in vain. For example, a safari park may only be open during the warmer months and a 'Last entry' and 'Park closes' time given. Some attractions, such as Granada Studios Tour, are not available on certain days because filming is taking place then.

Most leaflets and advertisements carry some indication of the price, with a note of any reduction for children, families, pre-booked parties and people on pensions.

Facilities are also listed in the leaflets: there is usually a shop, toilets with disabled access and somewhere to change a baby; somewhere to eat and drinks, snacks, ice-cream and perhaps a café available.

Services offered are car parking, first-aid post, brochures and maps to help people to find their way round the attraction, lost children post, picnic areas, seating and perhaps a playground for children.

Special events are advertised in the press and on television, such as the Edinburgh Tattoo, where the Lone Piper is seen playing a lament on the battlements of the castle.

Some attractions and special events have a commentary in

different languages, either by using audio equipment or by having guides who can speak several languages. The influx of visitors from the Far East has been recognised by the Beatrix Potter's Lake District Exhibition, which has a commentary in Japanese.

Visitors will find leaflets about attractions and places of interest in their hotels, guesthouses and self-catering accommodation, as well as in the local Tourist Information Centre, so that excursions can easily be planned from the information available.

ACTIVITY 3

Write out the following sentences, filling in the missing word(s).

1 Visitors need to know the _____ of places which they propose to visit.

2 Most visitors will use _____ transport and there are signs on the motorway to guide them to the location.

3 Tourists need to know when an attraction is _____.

4 Prices charged usually have a _____ for children, groups or families.

5 Special events may be advertised in the _____ and on _____.

ACTIVITY 4

Work in a small group. Ask your tutor to observe your discussion.

1 Imagine you are going to be the hosts for a day visit from students in a college in the next town. Discuss what interesting attractions exist in your area which the students might like to see. Make a list of all the suggestions.

2 Choose one or two of the suggestions to be the basis of a day's activities. Suggest the information needs which your visitors will have. Make a list of these needs.

3 If the visitors were to stay for two days, what other needs will they have? Discuss these and make a list.

4 Make out your own individual list of suggestions. Ask your tutor to observe your discussion and to sign your individual list of suggestions.

ACTIVITY 5

Work in pairs.

1 Choose local attractions for (a) a one-day visit, and (b) a two-day visit from other students in a college in the next town. Find out about:

- ▶ the event or attraction
- ▶ when it is open
- ▶ where it is located
- ▶ what transport is needed
- ▶ how much it will cost
- ▶ what facilities are available (i.e. snack bar, parking, etc.)
- ▶ any special services available (i.e. a guide).

2 On computer, draw up a programme with this information for:

(a) a one-day visit
(b) a two-day visit with overnight accommodation.

You may wish to use a facility such as your local youth hostel for accommodation at a reasonable cost. You will find details under 'Youth Hostels Association' in the Phone Book.

ACTIVITY 6

In 1992 the number of visitors from the UK was 10,364 and the number of tourists from overseas was 7,783 (source: Regional Trends 1994). To work out the percentage of overseas to UK visitors, do the following.

1 Use a calculator with a percentage button:

Enter 7,783
Press ÷
Enter 10,364
Press %

If your calculator does not have a percentage button:

Enter 7,783
Press ÷

Enter 10,364
Press ×
Enter 100
Press =

2 Write down your answer to two decimal points.

CORE SKILLS: *Application of number 1.1 PC 1, 2, 3, 4: (using simple percentages)*

3 Write out the following sentence, filling in the missing blank with the percentage you have just calculated:

In 1992, the percentage of overseas to UK visitors was _____%.

Types of information materials

Advertisements to promote tourist attractions are found on TV, on local radio and in newspapers, magazines and journals. Written advertisements use an eye-catching headline, with a picture which illustrates what is being offered. If the organisation is well known, it will have a logo which is used in the advertisement. Words such as 'free!', 'special offer!', 'buy now!' attract the reader's attention.

Travel advertisements use plenty of adjectives to describe the destination, e.g. magnificent, exotic, sandy palm-fringed beaches (words which make you long to visit that particular spot!) The information is not given in sentences but in short, snappy phrases, as people tend to glance quickly at advertisements and the information must be put in a way which can easily be taken in.

Leaflets and brochures

A visit to your local library, Tourist Information Centre or travel agency will provide plenty of examples of leaflets and brochures. There is more scope in a leaflet than in a newspaper advertisement for giving information about the amenity.

Posters and notices

Like advertisements, posters and notices need a large eye-catching headline to attract attention and a short, simple message. The writer of a notice has to put it where the people it is intended for will see it (perhaps in the window of a travel agency), and sometimes the writer cannot tell if the notice has been a success or not.

Handout

The first reaction of someone who is given a handout is to look at it quickly to see if it is of interest: the second is to keep it to look at again, or to look for a waste-paper basket and throw it in. It is important to get the reader's attention quickly: 'Children go free!', 'Two for the price of one!' may persuade the reader to find out more.

Case study

Peter and Hannah had worked in both large and small hotels for 15 years when they were left a legacy. After some discussion, they decided to open up a small hotel which had eight bedrooms, a dining room, a lounge, kitchen and a staff flat where they would live.

In order to keep the work to a level which they could manage themselves, they decided to offer bed-and-breakfast to their guests and to use the dining room as a café each afternoon. The hotel was in a small pretty village which attracted tourists from many nearby towns. At weekends, the café was very busy as people from the surrounding area came to the village. During the week, visiting business people booked in for bed-and-breakfast.

One day, a coach stopped outside the hotel and the driver came in to ask if Peter and Hannah could do afternoon tea for 50 people, there and then! Fortunately they were able to take up the challenge.

After the coach party had left, Peter and Hannah decided that it might be a good idea to offer afternoon tea to visiting tourists who came in a large party and began to make their plans.

ACTIVITY 7

Answer the following questions in full sentences.

1 What experiences would help Peter and Hannah to make a success of their new hotel?

2 What two things did they decide to do to keep costs down?

3 Which people were the overnight guests?

4 Where did the tourists come from at weekends?

5 How do you think Peter and Hannah would advertise their new idea of afternoon tea for coach parties?

6 What kind of tourists would make up a visiting coach party – local or from abroad?

7 How might Peter and Hannah get in touch with these people, without spending a great deal of money on advertising?

CORE SKILL: *Communication 1.2 Produce written material*
PC 1, 2, 3, 4
Range 1, 2, 3 (outline), 4

ACTIVITY 8

Visit your local tourist information centre, library, travel agent or visitors' centre and collect some information materials. Obtain at least one from each of the following types:

▶ leaflets
▶ posters (possibly about special events)
▶ advertisements
▶ notices (timetables for transport, list of opening times).

You may also use newspapers, journals and magazines for advertisements.

Many local newspapers carry full-page advertisements at holiday times on 'What to Do and Where to Go'. Travel agents send newsletters off to their regular customers with information about the latest developments and at holiday times advertise on TV. Some attractions advertise on TV for most of the year so that they keep in the public eye. Local commercial radio also has suggestions for visitors. Tourist board brochures also advertise events.

Sports and leisure centres also advertise special courses, particularly in the school holidays, and these can be found at the centre itself, in the library and in the local newspaper.

ACTIVITY 9

Work in pairs.

1 Visit your local tourist information centre, library, town hall, visitors' centre, travel agent and ask for examples of printed materials (such as brochures or advertisements) for local visitor attractions. Information about coming theatre attractions, concerts, sports events may be available.

2 Write a short account of the way in which one of these examples would be used to inform visitors to the area about the events.

ACTIVITY 10

Work in pairs.

1 Look back at your programme for a one-day or two-day visit from students at another college see Activity (5) and choose one of the attractions on the programme.

2 Visit the attraction and check up on all the details for the programme – the times it is open, the cost, the facilities and services available. If possible, take some photographs of each other enjoying the facilities. Keep the photographs to use in the next element.

Evidence indicator

1 Collect the information which you have obtained during this element about the provision of visitor information in your local area. You may find a brochure on your particular area useful.

2 From your information, decide if your area caters for the main four types of visitor:

- adults
- families
- UK-based
- from outside the UK.

Decide which attractions would suit each type of visitor.

3 Choose six examples of information needs of visitors from:

- locations
- times
- prices
- availability
- facilities
- events
- services
- attractions.

Match those needs to types of visitor. For example, you may decide that families need information about prices for family groups and where the attraction is located.

4 Look at the four examples of types of information materials shown:

- posters
- leaflets
- advertisements
- notices.

Using the examples you have collected, or other examples which are suited, describe the types of information materials used by visitors to the local area. For example, you may use a poster giving details of a concert or play at a local theatre.

5 People who visit an area often obtain information from a brochure or a book about the area, or from articles or advertisements in the press or on TV. Choose two main

sources of information about your local area which are used to inform visitors. Write a short account of how your sources give information to visitors.

Evaluation

1 Check through your work and state if your information is correct and that everything you were asked to do has been done.

2 Is your work presented to the highest standards of neatness and tidiness?

3 State the good ideas which you used in this unit.

4 Write about the ideas which didn't work, or which you decided not to use, and say why you didn't use them.

5 Think about ways in which you could improve your work and write them down.

Revision and specimen test questions

Focus 4: Local visitor information materials

Reference: Element 2.2 PC1, PC2, PC3, PC4, PC5

External test requirements

a *Identify the main types of visitor participating in leisure and tourism activities in a given local area.*
b *Identify examples of the most common information needs which visitors have for information about a given local area.*

Range

Main types of visitors: adults, families; UK-based, from outside the UK. Common information needs of visitors: locations, times, prices, availability, facilities, events, services, attractions

Main types of visitors include those travelling for business purposes, adults and families who may be UK-based or come from outside the UK. If they are travelling with a tour operator, they may have a programme of visits and things to do. If they are deciding on their own visits, they will need to see maps of their destination and find road signs showing the location. They need to know the times an attraction is open and if it is available for the whole year. Leaflets usually give information about facilities and services. Special events (such as the Jorvik Viking Festival) are advertised in the press and at Tourist Information Centres.

1 There are many top visitor attractions in London. Which of the following visitors would be most likely to visit these attractions in a visit lasting two or three days?
   a theatregoers attending a matinée by coach from Leeds
   b sales people at a one-day conference
   c residents of London
   d visitors from abroad

2 Which two types of visitors are most likely to stay in the seaside resort of Llandudno in Wales during the month of August?
   1 business travellers
   2 UK-based residents
   3 families with children
   4 backpackers from Australia

   Choose from:
   a 1 and 2
   b 2 and 3
   c 3 and 4
   d 1 and 4

3 Which two of the following pieces of information would visitors to Edinburgh in Scotland need to know?
   1 how to get there
   2 what attractions and events are available
   3 where to find heather-covered hills
   4 whether 'the haggis' is a small animal

   Choose from:
   a 1 and 2
   b 2 and 3
   c 3 and 4
   d 1 and 4

4 A business visitor to a conference at a seaside hotel in Brighton would need to know:
   a how much a visit to the nearest children's theme park would be
   b if the weather was going to be fine
   c what car parking facilities were available
   d if the hotel provided cots and high-chairs for babies

External test requirements

c *Recognise descriptions and identify examples of the types of information materials used for visitors to a given local area.*

Range

Types of information materials: leaflets, posters, advertisements, notices

Types of information materials match the size of the attraction and the number of visitors expected. For example, Thorpe Park would advertise on television. This is an expensive way of advertising but is suitable for places wishing to attract thousands of visitors. A small working farm hoping to attract people who are staying in the area would have leaflets printed and put in local accommodation, libraries and the tourist information centre. They would probably take an advertisement in the brochure published by their area tourist board. Notices and posters are also cheap and would be placed where visitors would see them as they move about the area.

5 Information about accommodation, places of interest, attractions, events, facilities and articles about a local tourist area is called a:
   a leaflet
   b brochure
   c magazine
   d journal

6 Visitors staying in a guesthouse in a holiday area would be most likely to find information about smaller attractions in the area from:

a television advertisements
b computer print-outs
c leaflets
d a national magazine

External test requirements

d *Identify the main sources of information materials for visitors in a given local area.*

Range

Main sources: tourist information centres, visitor information centres, libraries, town halls

Most town centres have signs pointing to their tourist information centre, whose telephone number and address may be found in the Phone Book, or there may be a visitor information centre instead. The town hall may also have information for visitors, as the local authority runs many recreational and leisure pursuits. Other sources are the local library.

7 A couple wishing to take a holiday in Great Yarmouth would be most likely to write for information about the area to:

a the local newspaper
b the tourist information centre at the resort

c their own library
d *Yellow Pages* directory

8 A family taking a four-day break in York would most likely obtain information about local events and attractions from the:

a cathedral
b posters in their own town
c local shops
d visitor information centre

External test requirements

e *Recognise descriptions and identify examples of media used to inform visitors in a given local area.*

Range

Media: press, printed materials, radio, TV

Local and national newspapers carry advertisements and information about holidays: the relevant tourist board produces brochures, local radio gives information and large attractions advertise on television.

9 An advertisement to inform visitors about an open-air play in a holiday area would most likely appear in:

a a television advertisement
b a theatre notice board
c the local newspaper
d a travel agent's window

element 2.3

Draft information leaflets for incoming visitors

Types of visitor attractions

Visitor attractions can be divided into:

- recreation
- culture and entertainment
- children's attractions.

Local attractions are likely to be provided by the local authority and may include:

- libraries
- museums and art galleries
- community centres
- parks and playgrounds
- sports fields and swimming pools
- recreation and sports halls
- theatres and concert halls.

The British Museum in London.

The Department of National Heritage is involved in national activities and the responsibilities include:

- broadcasting
- the film industry
- sports
- the arts
- heritage and tourism.

Help is offered to develop and improve facilities, e.g. theatres can apply to the Arts Council for grants to help to fund their work.

Children's attractions include theme parks (which are similar to Disneyworld) and provide a range of rides aimed at families and teenagers. The visitor can have as many rides as he or she wants after paying an entry fee. These parks also have catering facilities, car parks, services (such as first-aid) and toilets. Zoos and safari parks also attract children and families. Holiday centres (such as Center Parcs) offer accommodation and a covered leisure pool with other activities which is very popular with children. There are also variations on the ordinary swimming pool which have waterslides and wave machines that children enjoy. Seaside resorts which once relied on the weather now have covered attractions, where children can play happily in warm temperatures however cold, rainy and unpleasant it is outside.

ACTIVITY 1

Work in pairs.

The requirements for this element are that students should choose one local and one national attraction and design a leaflet for each of them.

Think of some attractions both local and national and make a list of these. Make sure you have included all three classes:

- recreation
- culture and entertainment
- children's attractions.

For information on the top ten historic properties and their number of visitors last year, you may wish to send off to:

The British Tourist Authority
Thames Tower
Black's Road
LONDON
W6 9EL

One of these attractions may be useful for making a leaflet for a national attraction.

Types of leaflets

When designing a leaflet you need to consider your intended audience (in other words, who your customers will be!). National attractions may be the ballet, stately homes, heritage centres, historic places of interest which will be visited by people resident in the UK and tourists from abroad. Some of these people will have limited English so the leaflet must have simple, easy to read language and use maps, pictures and signs.

Although you may be aiming at children with your leaflet, don't forget that although they have the 'pester power', it is the adults who decide whether to go or not, so your leaflet must

Children have the 'pester power' but adults have to pay.

include all the information necessary for adults to make a decision.

The leaflet may be a classy, glossy, colourful affair, if it is for an attraction which would appeal to thousands of people. If it is for a local audience (e.g. a leaflet detailing information about a local authority leisure centre and swimming pool in the school holidays, to be used for a limited time), it would probably be done with a desk-top publishing package.

The Advertising Standards Authority receives any complaints about advertisements which do not live up to the standard of being legal, decent, honest and truthful. This basic guideline must be followed in any advertisement.

The advantages of leaflets are that they are fairly cheap to produce and they can be taken away and studied. Colour printing, pictures and photographs may be used to make them more attractive.

ACTIVITY 2

Work in a small group or in pairs.

1 Collect some newspaper or magazine advertisements to see how they are set out. What made you notice them in the first place? Write down any good ideas which you like about the advertisements.

2 Start to collect a selection of leaflets from various attractions and bring them to your next session.

Appropriate information

A leaflet needs to have significant and up-to-date information appropriate to the intended audience. 'Significant' means vital information – things which people *must* know before they can decide to choose to go to the attraction. Is parking available? What does it cost? Where is it? What are the opening hours? Of course, the information must be checked by visiting or telephoning to make sure that it is correct. Some attractions may only be open in the summer whilst others, such as theatres, will have extra performances in the afternoons during the Christmas holidays.

Work with the same people as for Activity 2.

1 Discuss your favourite sport or recreational activity.

2 Imagine that you have agreed to try the favourite sport of each member of the group or, if this is not possible, you have agreed to go and watch.

Each person now draws up a list of instructions which can be used by the other members of the group to take part in (or watch) a recreational activity. Decide what to include in your list. Word process the list and make a copy for each of the other members.

3 Take each list in turn and decide whether you could take part in or watch the activity from the information given.

If there are any improvements or additions, make them to the information on disk and print a second copy to attach to the first.

Following someone else's instructions can help you to decide what to put in your own leaflet so that people can use it easily. If you decide to put the idea into practice and take part in each other's interests, using the list of instructions as a guide, you could have an enjoyable time.

When you are thinking about the attraction you will make a leaflet for, you will need to consider:

▶ who the attraction's existing customers are
▶ what these customers need or want
▶ where the customers come from
▶ what level of prices the customers will accept for the services
▶ the good or bad points about the attraction.

You will need to think about gathering information to go on the leaflet. You will need to consider:

▶ how to get there
▶ entrance prices
▶ group rates
▶ concessions
▶ accommodation
▶ catering
▶ disabled visitors
▶ provision for dogs
▶ restrictions (i.e. height restrictions for children)
▶ opening times (summer, winter, late nights)
▶ security
▶ first-aid

- telephones
- toilets
- baby supplies
- cash dispensers
- souvenir shops
- parking for cars and coaches
- sketch map or plan
- indoor or all-weather attractions.

You may find that it is difficult to judge what to put in and what to leave out! You may find that it is easier to word process all the material and then cut and paste it into position, particularly if your leaflet is going to be more than two sides of A4.

Remember that reprographics can enlarge or reduce your lettering and pictures so that you can use different sizes of print.

ACTIVITY 4

Work in pairs or in a small group.

1 Go through the list of ideas for attractions you made in Activity 1. Discuss the advantages and disadvantages of each attraction in turn, and write these down next to each attraction. Save this information for your evaluation at the end of the assignment.

2 Choose a local and a national attraction for the leaflets you are going to create.

Language and layout

A leaflet which has simple language will be read and understood easily by children and by foreign visitors whose English is limited. Pictures and sketch maps are helpful. When you plan your leaflet, you may need the help of an Information Technology specialist so that you can use the painting and drawing techniques of a graphics package. This can assist you to create a leaflet which looks as if it has come straight from the printer!

Planning

Work in pairs or in a small group.

1 Read through the information on creating a leaflet which follows this activity.

2 Write down a plan of how you will work on the leaflet, which jobs need doing and who will do them. Estimate how long the jobs will take.

3 Plan your research for ideas (i.e. looking at the leaflets and advertisements you have collected).

4 Make a list of any equipment or materials you will need. Plan when you will use the equipment and book it if necessary.

5 Plan when you will have the rough draft ready for checking with your tutor.

6 Make individual copies of the plan.

When you create a leaflet, you will need to consider:

The front page:

▶ the title – this is often the name of the attraction
▶ a sentence which makes the customer want to know more
▶ an eye-catching picture of part of the attraction
▶ a sentence to make it clear whether it is for adults, families or both.

The inside pages:

▶ details of the attraction: rides, scenes, wildlife
▶ map or sketch showing how to move around it
▶ photo or picture of someone enjoying it!
▶ names of displays to be seen
▶ if it is an all-weather attraction.

The back page:

▶ how to get there – perhaps with a map
▶ name, address and telephone number
▶ when it is open
▶ admission prices and what the price covers
▶ how payment can be made: (Access, Visa, cash or cheques)
▶ any special concessions (children, groups, pensioners)
▶ special facilities (for disabled, babies, children)
▶ parking facilities and transport other than cars
▶ facilities for dogs.

The leaflet should:

▶ make the customer want to go there
▶ tell the customer as much as possible about the attraction
▶ give information about how to get there with directions from motorways.

Work in pairs or in a small group.

1 Create the first leaflet for a local attraction. Start by drafting your leaflet. Look at a graphics or desk-top publishing package and plan any pictures which will look good on your leaflet. You may have some photographs taken in the last unit which would be useful.

2 Look back at the information which might go on a leaflet and pick out what you think should go on yours. Make a draft copy either by hand or on the word processor. Decide on the size of the leaflet. If you use A4, will you fold it?

An A4 leaflet with information on both sides will look like this:

The printer should be set for 'landscape'.

Each person should decide which part of the leaflet to produce.

3 Check the wording on your leaflet by using the spell-check, then ask your tutor to look it over.

4 Make any necessary revisions. Ask another group of students to exchange leaflets with you. Check each other's leaflets for mistakes and anything which might have been left out.

5 Revise the leaflet if necessary and then print out one copy for each person in the group and an extra copy for printing.

CORE SKILLS: *Information Technology 1.2 PC 1, 2, 3 and 5*

Many schools and colleges have a Reprographics Department which produces leaflets, information about courses and other printing materials. Your leaflet will probably be suitable for reproducing in this way. For the moment, put the printed copy to one side.

Work in pairs or in a small group.

1 Choose a national attraction for which you are going to produce a leaflet to be professionally printed. A large national attraction would appeal to tourists from

outside the UK as well as UK-based visitors, so this leaflet could be aimed at a large audience.

2 Make up another leaflet, using a graphics package if possible for the lettering and

information, and photographs for illustrations. Glossy paper is often used and maybe a map which shows the location of the nearest big towns or cities and motorways clearly marked. The leaflet could carry a slogan in more than one language to appeal to international visitors: 'Welcome!', 'Bienvenue!', 'Welkommen!'.

3 Check the leaflet carefully and as before, ask another student group and your tutor to glance at it.

4 Print a draft copy and then a final copy for each of you, with an extra final copy for the printer.

ACTIVITY 8

1 Take your first leaflet (from Activity 6) to your Reprographics Department.
   a Find out what it would cost to produce 100 leaflets, printed both sides. Check whether the price would include folding the leaflets.
   b Ask if there would be a difference in price for white or coloured paper.
   c Ask if the copying facility can copy colours.

2 When you have the answers to these questions, write down what it would cost to produce:
   a 100 leaflets on (i) white paper, and (ii) coloured paper.

b 1000 leaflets on (i) white paper, and (ii) coloured paper.

3 Imagine that, as designers, students were paid £5.00 per hour to create the leaflet. Make an estimate of how much your time would cost. Add this to the cost of the leaflet.

4 a Divide by 100 to find the cost each of 100 leaflets.
   b Divide by 1000 to find the cost each of 1000 leaflets.

CORE SKILLS: *Application of number 1.2 Estimate*
PC 1, 2, 3
Range 2

ACTIVITY 9

Get a price estimate for the second leaflet (from Activity 7) from a professional printer, if possible. The school or college will probably use a printer for letter headings, brochures or other school materials. Enquire at your school or college office to find out if there is a printer used by your educational establishment who would give you an estimated price for printing **a** 100, and **b** 1000 leaflets.

If you have no connection with a printer, write letters to one or two printers taken from

Yellow Pages or other directories. Explain that you are researching information for a school or college leisure and tourism project and that you need an estimated price for producing **a** 100, and **b** 1000 copies of the enclosed leaflet.

When you get a reply, remember to write and thank the printer for the time and trouble which has been taken.

CORE SKILL: *Application of number 1.1 Collect*
and record data

PC 1, 2, 3, 4
Range 3 (Units of money)

If a letter is written:

Communication 1.2 Produce written

material
PC 1, 2, 3, 4 (information to suit a purpose)
Range 1, 2, 3 (outline)

ACTIVITY 10

Write out the following sentences, filling in the missing word(s).

1 When writing a leaflet, students should consider the intended audience; in other words, who the _____ will be.

2 If the people who are going to read the leaflet have limited English, _____ will help them to understand the leaflet.

3 Children may be the persuaders when families visit an attraction, but the decision whether to go or not is usually made by the _____.

4 The Advertising Standards Authority wants all advertisements to be legal, decent, _____ and truthful.

5 The word 'significant' means _____ information – things which people must know about an attraction.

6 Using Information Technology will help to create a leaflet which looks as if it has come from a _____.

Evidence indicator

1 Using the leaflet for a local attraction which you have produced (from Activity 6) explain:
   a who the intended audience is.
   b why you chose that particular attraction.
   c what you did to suit the leaflet to the intended customer.
   d how you arrived at the production costs.
   e what it cost per leaflet for **i** 100, and **ii** 1000 copies.
   f why there is a difference in production costs when more leaflets are printed.

2 Using the leaflet for a national attraction which you have produced (from Activity 7) explain:
   a who the intended audience is.
   b why this leaflet is different to the one for the local attraction.
   c what makes this leaflet suitable for its intended customers.

d how you arrived at the production costs.

e what it cost per leaflet for **i** 100, and **ii** 1000 copies.

3 Suggest some local places where yo u would make the leaflets available.

Evaluation

1 Look at the action plan you made for this unit.

Write down the alternatives you thought about when deciding to do this leaflet.

2 Write down why you chose the alternative you used and the reasons why you chose not to use other methods.

3 Can you think of any improvements which you could make?

Revision and specimen test questions

Focus 5: Information leaflets

Reference: Element 2.3 PC1, PC2, PC3, PC5, PC6

External test requirements

a *Recognise significant information appropriate for inclusion in an information leaflet for a given visitor attraction and a given audience.*

Range

Visitor attractions: local, national; recreation, culture and entertainment, children's attractions

Intended audience: visitors from other parts of the UK, visitors from outside the UK, visitors with limited English; adults, families

Significant information: main features, products and services, transport access, location, prices

Visitor attractions at local level will include local authority provision, such as playgrounds, parks, museums, art galleries, libraries, theatre and concert halls, sports fields and sports halls, swimming pools and recreational and community centres.

National attractions include national parks, the arts, historical and heritage centres, sports, radio and television, the film industry.

Children's attractions are theme parks, zoos, holiday centres, swimming and activity pools, all-weather attractions.

1 Which two of the following would visitors to *The Sandcastle* at Blackpool most likely expect to see on the leaflet?
   1 how many people it holds
   2 how much it costs to enter
   3 where to park the car
   4 what jobs are available there

   Choose from:
   a 1 and 2
   b 2 and 3
   c 3 and 4
   d 1 and 4

2 Visitors from abroad wishing to spend some time in the Lake District National Park would need to know:
   a who the owners are
   b how many lakes there are
   c where the farmers live
   d if accommodation is available

3 Families from the UK plan to visit a safari park during the Easter holidays. Which two of the following would they most likely need to know about?
   1 where it is located
   2 what date the park is open to the public
   3 how many animals it contains
   4 what languages the staff can speak

   Choose from:
   a 1 and 2
   b 2 and 3
   c 3 and 4
   d 1 and 4

External test requirements

b *Recognise how given resources can best be used to produce a leaflet, and relate resources to given production costs.*

Range

Resources: materials, time, finance, skills

Production costs: preparation, print (print run, size, layout, completion of content)

When considering the costs of information leaflets, the time taken to prepare them, the amount to be produced and the information included must be worked out. Once the leaflet has been put together the unit cost of each leaflet goes down when large amounts are printed.

4 Which of the following would be the least costly way to produce information for a summer programme at a local authority leisure centre to reach the maximum number of people?
   a desk-top publishing photocopied leaflet
   b handwritten leaflet individually produced
   c one notice in coloured paint outside the centre
   d a handwritten note pinned up at the ticket kiosk

5 Which of the following would be the best way to produce a leaflet intended to inform visitors about a large zoo?
   a a typed leaflet with text but no pictures
   b a picture using felt-tips
   c a glossy professionally printed leaflet
   d a competition for under-7s

Investigating working in the leisure and tourism industries

Investigate the leisure and tourism industries

The UK leisure and recreation industry

Leisure can be described as the absence of work, although when we do something like helping with a youth organisation or raising funds for our favourite charity, we may spend our leisure time in a very similar way to someone else's working day!

Leisure is the freedom to do what we *want* to do, rather than doing something which we *must* do. We have the opportunity of using spare time in a way which appeals to us. Free time is that which is left over from working, or because we are on holiday, or have retired from work.

Recreation may be defined as amusement, entertainment, playing sports, finding something to do which suits the person. The leisure and recreation business is developing rapidly as people make an effort to keep fit by taking part in a sport. This gives a person the opportunity to meet others and there is enjoyment in doing this.

New leisure complexes have been built which contain swimming pools with water chutes and a tropical atmosphere, a multigym, solarium, squash courts and working-out with weights. The weather may not matter to people taking part in the traditional sporting activities of swimming, sailing, riding and walking.

ACTIVITY 1

Work in groups of 2 to 4 people.

1 Make a list of all the leisure activities you can think of.

2 After five minutes, the groups stop making lists. Someone from the first group reads out everything on their list. If the activity appears on the lists made by other groups, they are ticked.

3 A person from the second group then reads out any activities not on the first list, and these are ticked. This continues until all the activities thought of by the whole group have been covered.

Did the groups think of places like zoos, safari parks and theme parks, and indoor activities (such as five-a-side football, indoor tennis, trampolines)? Work-out facilities may be offered in places like hotels; roller- or ice-skating rinks, art galleries, libraries and museums are also leisure activities.

Arts and entertainment

Theatres and concert halls are usually situated in the centres of towns and some large arenas (like the Nynex Arena in Manchester) are used for concerts, ice-skating displays, rock bands, pop groups and other entertainments.

ACTIVITY 2

Look in *Yellow Pages*, *Thomson* directory, your local newspaper or contact your local tourist information centre. Obtain information about the theatres, cinemas and concert halls in your locality. Find out what events will take place in the near future and make a list. Use a word processor for your list and if possible include the telephone number to ring in order to book seats.

Outdoor activities

Many outdoor activities are offered in the local parks. You may find that your local park offers:

- bowling
- riding
- golf
- tennis courts
- football pitches
- walks or nature trails
- children's playground.

These are all run by your local authority.

National Sports Centres may offer formal training courses for outdoor activities. Your tourist information centre will have information which promotes walking, fishing and sailing as outdoor activities.

Outdoor pursuits centres offer canoeing, hiking and mountain climbing. You may also have a country park in your area or a local centre for water sports.

The natural resources of an area (such as beautiful scenery, lakes, countryside, mountains or hills) lend themselves to certain outdoor activities.

ACTIVITY 3

1 Choose an outdoor location wherever you like (in your local area or in another region which you know well). Find out which centres of population are within a radius of about 50 miles from the facility.

2 Find out whether there is public transport to the location or whether the users go there by car or by coach.

3 Give as many reasons for the popularity of the outdoor location as you can think of.

4 Write a short account of your findings.

Sports spectating

Many people follow sports as spectators: football, rugby and cricket clubs, indoor tennis, squash, badminton and skating all have spectator facilities. Viewing sport is a favourite leisure activity.

Action sport

Energetic people can find plenty of potential in the leisure industry to satisfy their craving for adventure. They can choose from downhill skiing or the martial arts and self-defence, climbing and mountaineering, hang-gliding or para-gliding, water sports, hiking and lightweight camping.

Sports products and services

Sports need equipment and traditional dress, and there are many specialist shops which provide these, often with an assistant who is knowledgeable in the field. Famous football teams sell replicas of the team 'strip', in both child and adult sizes, together with scarves and badges which spectators use to identify with their team.

There are snack bars, cafés and shops which offer services to those looking for the social aspect as well as those who partake in sport. Coaches and instructors give training from the basic to the advanced, if that is required, or the facility can be used for fun.

There are work duties in taking bookings for the facility, putting out and taking in the equipment, supervising the customers and making sure they are safe. A service offered to Big Business is to take out and test would-be company managers for leadership and initiative, and someone offers the service of assessing them.

Sports centres

Sports and leisure centres are offered in both the public and private sectors because this growing business is seen as promoting health and fitness, as well as catering for hobbies and giving amusement. Sports centres run by the local authority may offer swimming pools, squash courts, multigym, climbing walls, trampolines, badminton and other activities. Private sports centres also attract people who want to keep fit and may be found in new hotel developments, offering weight-training equipment and saunas.

1 As a group, brainstorm and write down all the local sports and leisure facilities you can think of, including those in nearby towns.

2 Divide into groups of 3 or 4 people, and each take a different centre if possible. Arrange to visit a sports centre (telephone first). Ask if it is possible for someone to answer your questions, and devise a questionnaire to find out:

   a who manages or is responsible for the centre.
   b how many full-time and part-time employees there are.
   c if there are any voluntary workers.
   d if there are any coaches employed by the centre.
   e if there are any coaches or instructors who hire the facilities for their own groups.
   f what sports or activities are offered.
   g if there are any catering facilities.
   h how people book the facilities.
   i if there are any special courses offered.
   j if there are any special offers for school children in the holidays.

3 From the information you have gathered, write an individual account of the sports centre you visited.

Heritage

Our history and heritage is about ordinary people and their work in the past which has helped to shape the kind of people we are. Keeping history alive is now big business and our stately homes, monuments, museums and art galleries are a big draw to tourists both from the UK and from abroad.

More than 52,000,000 people paid visits to heritage sites last year to see the sites of old battlefields, look at famous houses and castles, or see the collections of famous paintings and treasures which are contained in them.

The government, through English Heritage and the Scottish Office, is responsible for looking after ruins and castles. The National Trust looks after all kinds of buildings, and an organisation called the Historic Houses Association offers help to private owners.

Many large houses have parks and estates surrounding them and conservation work is done to keep the grounds, the walls, the lakes and waterways and the gardens in good order. Some great houses have an interesting feature in the grounds – a bird sanctuary or a pets' corner – to attract the visitors.

There are centres (such as Quarry Bank Mill in Cheshire) which show how people lived and worked years ago, and museums which show industrial machinery at work. At Wigan Pier, neglected warehouses on the side of the canal have been transformed into a history museum. There is a Victorian school room, with a strict teacher! Children who visit can join the actors to experience life in school a hundred years ago.

ACTIVITY 5

Work in groups of 2 to 4 people.

1 Choose an example of a historical attraction, an industrial heritage museum or a monument. Find out what goods or services are supplied to the visitors – is there a shop, a café or a guide? Is the visitor able to buy a souvenir to take home?

2 Write an individual short account of the goods and services which are needed by visitors to the attraction.

Play

The local authority usually provides play areas in the local parks and also offers supervised play schemes, craft sessions and sporting activities in the long school holidays, often using school premises.

Many tourist attractions have an adventure playground or activity centre for the children who visit and these are very much enjoyed. Ideally, a children's playground should be fenced off, have wood chip or other safe surfaces underneath the equipment and be free from hazards.

Private companies also offer supervised holiday activities for children of different ages, in a weekly or fortnightly programme. Besides regular staff, instructors and coaches, they often employ seasonal workers (such as students) to help to look after the children.

Voluntary organisations (such as the Scout Association, the Boys' Brigade, the Guide Association or Woodland Folk) offer activities to young people who are supervised by trained adult helpers. Other volunteers may run local sports clubs or youth football teams.

Large theme parks offer activities for the whole family and are very popular with visitors, but they are expensive to set up. They often charge admission but all the rides in the park are free. Such places can be very crowded at peak times and young people may not be able to do all the activities they would wish.

1 Choose a facility for play activities in your own locality, or in another area if you prefer.

2 Describe the facility.

3 Write a short account of **a** the good things about it, and **b** the bad things about it, from the point of view of a young person using it.

Catering

Catering is providing food for people. It can range from the hot-dog stall to the five-star restaurant, and all kinds of meals in between. The catering services offered in places which attract day visitors are often quite basic – fast food or snacks provided by part-time, temporary staff who have been engaged to cover the busy season. Many leisure and recreation facilities use the serve-yourself snack bar for their customers as this keeps the cost down.

However, restaurant meals are often an occasion to be enjoyed – maybe to celebrate a birthday or anniversary or to clinch a business deal. The service is more formal, with the waiter or waitress coming to the table to take the order and bring the food.

Work in groups of 2 to 4 people.

1 Brainstorm the catering facilities in a range of leisure facilities which you have visited or know about and make a list of them.

2 Choose four or five *different* catering facilities from the list. Decide:
   a was the catering enough for the customers?
   b was the price satisfactory?
   c was the service good or bad?
   d was the place reasonably clean and tidy?
   e would you recommend it to other people?

3 Write a short paragraph for each of the catering facilities stating whether you felt it was very good, good, fair, poor or bad.

Accommodation

Visitors may need to stay for one night or more in an area and they will need accommodation which can vary from the self-catering cottage or caravan, to a large hotel where everything is done for the customer.

In between these two extremes are the bed-and-breakfast places where the owner does all the work of booking, reception, cleaning, making the beds, cooking the breakfast and doing the accounts. There are small hotels where the workers have to be flexible and double-up on duties (such as the reception desk and waiting at the table). There are large hotels with separate staff for housekeeping and maintenance, reception and management, chefs and kitchen workers, each with their own job to do to make things run smoothly for the visitor.

Many people now take short breaks throughout the year as well as an annual holiday, so accommodation may be required all the time. Organisations may book hotel accommodation for their conferences, special activity weekends (e.g. for bridge players). Coach tours also book accommodation in different localities for their customers, who may come from the UK or from abroad. The needs for accommodation are growing. Some universities now offer their student accommodation and catering services when their students have gone home for their summer holiday.

ACTIVITY 8

Work in groups of 2 to 4 people.

1 Visit your local tourist information centre or contact a local hotel to find out whether accommodation costs the same during the week as it does at weekends.

2 Discuss your findings with other members of your group or with other groups and write a short account of what you find.

Use simple percentages (i.e. about 60%) to explain the proportion of hotels which charge less at weekends.

CORE SKILL: *Application of number 1.1 Collect and record data*
PC 1, 2, 3, 4
Range: Techniques (number) simple percentages

The UK travel and tourism industry

Travel services

Tourists who travel do so either by road, rail, sea or air or sometimes a combination of these. For example, in order to leave the UK a journey may still be made by road or rail using Le Shuttle to journey under the Channel. Passengers can take their vehicles aboard a ferry and use the facilities to have a meal or do some duty-free shopping. The quickest way to journey across different countries is to take an aeroplane.

Tourists may take their own vehicles to other countries or they may hire a car when they arrive. They may use local transport, such as buses and taxis or the railways and ferries.

Travel arrangements can be made through tour operators, travel agents or direct with the shipping or aeroplane company. Computers have made bookings simple, and electronic transfer of funds through credit and debit cards make it easy to pay for the travel services which can be booked over the telephone. Seats and space for vehicles can be reserved by rail or by sea, so that passengers can use their own vehicles when they arrive at their destinations.

ACTIVITY 9

Work in pairs.

Your group of students has decided to spend a three-day holiday in France. Find out:

a what flights to France are available.

b what ferry service you might use.
c when you could use Le Shuttle.
d if possible, the cost of the fare for an individual.

Incoming tours

There are three kinds of tour operators:

- those who take British people abroad
- those who bring foreign tourists to the UK
- those who sell domestic tours within Britain.

Tours of overseas visitors coming to the UK are usually very interested in our heritage. They may arrive by aeroplane and then use coaches to visit places (such as Holyrood House in Edinburgh and Stratford-upon-Avon). A tour which is being done as cheaply as possible may use university campus accommodation in the high season, when the students have gone home for the summer break. They may also use hotels, particularly at weekends when the price of a room is cheaper. Tourists are also interested in sporting facilities, culture and entertainment, shopping and fashion.

The tours are purchased in their own country, but once they reach the UK they spend money on goods and services as well as on accommodation and meals. In 1994, overseas visitors spent a total of £9,919 million on goods and services. Most of the goods were British-made, which helps the economy.

Outgoing tours

Outgoing tours are bought in the UK, usually from travel agents acting on behalf of tour operators, or as coach tours booked through and organised by a coach company. They are usually a package which includes travel, catering and accommodation, and some excursions or outings (which may be included in the price or may be extras).

The excursions usually include the services of a guide who can explain the historic connections of the places visited, or give interesting information about the attractions. The tour guide has to be able to cope with different age ranges and personalities and know how to handle of group of people.

Tourists, whether incoming or outgoing, can either:

- make bookings themselves with the various service providers
- ask a travel agent to make all the bookings

- buy a package tour already worked out by a tour operator.

The third option is usually the cheapest, as the tour operator can negotiate a lower price for full capacity. Most tours are sold through a brochure obtained through a travel agent, who gets commission from the tour operator.

Visitor attractions

On some tours, visits to attractions are included in the price, while on others, they are optional extras. Visitors may also decide to make their own way to an attraction, using their own transport, local buses or taxis. Information about these attractions is available on posters, information leaflets or brochures at the hotel. Some attractions are famous: visitors to London like to see the Tower, St Paul's Cathedral, the National History Museum and the Science Museum, and then Kew Gardens, the London parks and a look at Buckingham Palace and the Houses of Parliament.

Other attractions may be the result of an impulse visit on the part of the tourists to a place they didn't know existed.

Information services

Most local authorities in the UK hope to bring business into their area by promoting tourism. They need to attract business people, holiday-makers and day visitors. Hotels, leisure complexes, attractions, restaurants, cafés and pubs, shops and heritage centres are all publicised in brochures, leaflets and posters. Local guides and maps are placed in travel agents and in hotel receptions. Information can be obtained before a visit by contacting the local tourist information centre in the place where the visit is to be made.

The British Tourist Authority and the National Tourist Boards for England, Scotland and Wales are responsible for encouraging overseas and British tourists, and the provision of facilities and services for them. The Northern Ireland Tourist Board has a similar role. These Boards have order forms which detail their several publications and their addresses are:

British Tourist Authority and English Tourist Board
Thames Tower
Black's Road
LONDON
W6 9EL

Scottish Tourist Board
23 Ravelston Terrace
EDINBURGH
ET14 3EG

Wales Tourist Board
Brunel House
CARDIFF
CF2 1UY

Northern Ireland Tourist Board
St Anne's Court
59 North Street
BELFAST
BT1 1ND

🏃 🏃 🏃 🏃 🏃 **ACTIVITY 10** 🏃 🏃 🏃 🏃 🏃

_1_ Write to one of the tourist boards and ask for a guide to a particular region.

_2_ When you receive the guide, you may want to send off for further information about a particular area in that guide to use in your **Evidence indicator**.

Catering

Catering is the provision of food which may vary from the hot-dog stall in the street to a high-class restaurant. Snacks, ethnic food, pub grub and fast food outlets are all needed in a locality to suit the different needs of various visitors.

Accommodation

This is looking after people who are away from home for whatever reason and varies from bed-and-breakfast establishments to luxury hotels. Often hotels cater for the business visitor during the week and then at weekends for the short-break leisure visitor.

Some visitors prefer self-catering accommodation where they can make their own food. Families find this particularly convenient if there are small children who find it hard to sit still in a restaurant or café.

Transport

Many visitors like to have the convenience of their own cars in order to move about the area. Others use the local bus or train. Some steam trains have been revived and are used as a tourist attraction. Other transport may consist of a tractor ride round a farm or a coach trip to see a notable attraction. Visitors may like to hire a bicycle or a horse in order to look round the locality and others prefer to walk as part of their holiday.

ACTIVITY 11

Work in pairs.

Make a list of the local transport and telephone numbers where you can obtain more information that would be of use to a visitor.

Facilities

Leisure and recreation facilities

A **facility** is something which is provided for the visitor, such as catering and accommodation, car parking, information services, toilets. This costs the local authority money, which it hopes will be off-set by visitors spending money in the shops and attractions.

Theatres and concert halls, museums and heritage sites all offer leisure potential to visitors. The more active may prefer tracks, sports centres, swimming pools, activity centres, parks and play areas. Outdoor activities can be influenced by the weather. For example, the south usually has warmer summers than the north so people prefer to swim off the south coast rather than in the chilly north sea.

The location of various sporting activities owes much to the natural environment. Features such as lakes, hills and mountains attract people who wish to sail, windsurf or water-ski, or who want to walk on the fells or climb the mountains.

Visitors need something to eat and somewhere to stay, so catering establishments and accommodation of all types are to be found near to sports which use the natural environment.

Outdoor activities may be influenced by the weather.

Travel and tourism facilities

Travel agencies may have a section which caters for the business person and has a contract to provide accommodation for certain organisations. They know where to make bookings and save time and money for the organisation because they are experts.

In the same way, travel agencies also arrange holidays for tourists which can consist of booking flights only; booking a package tour with self-catering or hotel accommodation, arranging for airline tickets, travel insurance and car hire. They may also exchange money into the currency of the country the customer is travelling to. They can offer advice on the holiday resort – quiet, lively, noisy, out of the way. They remind the visitor of any inoculations required and if visas and passports are needed.

Package tours usually have transport arrangements, accommodation, the services of a guide or tour representative and information about visits to places of interest on the holiday. Short breaks are now becoming more popular. Once the customer has decided on the holiday, the travel agent uses a database to check that it is available and makes a booking.

Write out the following sentences, filling in the missing word(s).

1 Facilities such as _____ parking and catering are offered to visitors.

2 Outdoor activities can be _____ by the weather.

3 Sailing takes place where there is a feature of the natural environment such as a _____.

4 Travel agencies arrange holidays for _____.

5 Travel agents can offer _____ about the resort to which a tourist is going.

Work in pairs. Word process your information to use later in your **Evidence indicator**.

In this activity, you are going to look at the main components of the UK leisure and recreation industry nationally. You must give two examples of activities for each of the following components.

1 Visits to art centres and entertainment centres: theatres, concert halls, museums and art galleries.

2 Visits to heritage centres, places of historic interest.

3 Taking part in sports and sports spectating in sports centres, swimming pools and activity centres.

4 Taking part in outdoor activities, using areas with natural environmental features with leisure potential, such as hill walking, climbing, riding, canoeing, mountaineering.

5 Taking part in play activities in theme parks, play areas, activity centres.

Travel and tourism facilities are found through travel agencies and tour operators. The main travel principals are car-hire firms, airlines, railway and shipping companies, some of which are part of a large group of companies which own hotels as well. These large companies make up a large part of the holiday industry and have taken over many of the small tour operators. They also own many travel agents too which can lead to less competition within the holiday industry.

Work in pairs. Word process your information to use later in your **Evidence indicator**.

In this activity, you are going to look at the main components of UK travel and tourism nationally. Write a paragraph giving two examples of activities for each of the following components.

_1_ Travelling for pleasure (coach companies, tour operators operating visits to attractions).

_2_ Touring (coach holidays staying in different parts of the country).

_3_ Going on holiday.

_4_ Visiting attractions.

Two of the examples should include eating and drinking out.

Facilities in your locality

Your own locality will provide many leisure and recreation facilities which are used by the people who live there as well as visitors. These places will employ many people in various jobs, both seen and unseen, in order to keep the business going.

Besides the jobs directly created by the leisure industry, there is other work created: suppliers of food and drink, of souvenirs, those who print the leaflets, transport staff needed to take people to their leisure activity are all needed. Litter has to be removed, car park attendants appointed, toilet facilities provided. Some of this cost is borne by the local authority and passed on to the council tax payer. In areas where local residents are concerned about the effect of visitors on their environment, the local council may have to stabilise tourism if there are no positive advantages.

The leisure facilities in your own area will include theatres, concert halls, parks and museums, sports and activity centres, swimming pools, libraries, play areas, heritage and historical sites, and the catering and accommodation scene. You may have a large cinema complex nearby, fitness and leisure centres, sports training and coaching.

Travel and tourism facilities include airlines, car hire and ferry companies, travel agencies and tour operators, hotels, inns and catering services, tourist information centres (with perhaps a guide to local festival dates). They will also carry accommodation lists for hotels, etc.

🏃 🏃 🏃 🏃 🏃 **ACTIVITY 15** 🏃 🏃 🏃 🏃 🏃

Work in pairs.

You may combine your information but the final word-processed work must be done individually.

1 Collect information from your own locality which would be useful for a local guide to the area. Include information about sports participation and spectating, outdoor activities, play, travel, catering, accommodation and entertainment.

Include agency services (travel agent, tour operator) and information services (tourist information centre, local library or town hall).

2 Classify your information under headings such as:

- ▶ 'Days out'
- ▶ 'Nights out'
- ▶ 'Fun for the family'
- ▶ 'Sporting ideas'
- ▶ 'Travel around'
- ▶ 'Party time and catering'
- ▶ 'Industrial heritage'.

Add any other headings you can think of (the above headings are to be used as a guide and can be altered as you think fit).

People meet various needs in their leisure time. There is the need for entertainment, to interact socially with friends, to celebrate some event in our lives, to find new experiences, to meet challenges and to find personal satisfaction.

Many people give their leisure up to help others with their recreation. The uniformed youth organisations have leaders who spend their own time training to help young people, youth club leaders may work voluntarily, and school teachers take on the task of coaching the football team. This kind of activity can be a great source of personal satisfaction.

Many sports also have a social side to them – the cricket 'tea' after the game, the golf club dance – so that there are more recreational needs satisfied than would at first appear.

🏃 🏃 🏃 🏃 🏃 **ACTIVITY 16** 🏃 🏃 🏃 🏃 🏃

Look at the provision of leisure and tourism services in your own area. Make notes on how these satisfy your own needs for:

- ▶ physical activity
- ▶ social interaction
- ▶ a new experience
- ▶ a challenge
- ▶ personal satisfaction.

Evidence indicator

A brief report is required containing a general outline of the leisure and tourism industries nationally. The report should cover the main components of the leisure and recreation and the travel and tourism industries, with two examples of activities for each component.

1 Use the information from Activity 13. Set out your report in a formal manner with headings. The sections should contain the following information (the **terms of reference** has already been done for you).

- **Terms of reference** (A report on general outline of the leisure and tourism industries nationally.)
- **Method** (Here you will say that you chose two examples each of leisure and recreation and the travel and tourism industries. Then detail what you have chosen for numbers 1, 2, 3, 4 and 5 in Activity 13.)
- **Findings** (Here state the visits you suggested in Activity 13. You may be able to use the paragraphs which you already have on disk for this section.)
- **Conclusion** (Here you may summarise what you have found, e.g. you could put that there are varied and interesting examples of components of the leisure and recreation, travel and tourism industries.)

2 For the second part of this **Evidence indicator**, use the information from Activity 15 where you collected and classified information from your own locality. You may want to do this as a leaflet with a heading of: 'Local guide to Mosstown' (or whatever place you wish).

3 Finally, use your notes on the extent to which your own leisure and recreational needs are satisfied in your own locality.

4 Word process an account from these notes.

Evaluation

Look back at the way you planned your work.

1 Mention any good ideas.

2 Mention any alternatives which you used, and why you used them. Give the reasons you had for discarding ways of doing this work.

Revision and specimen test questions

Focus 1: Main components

Reference: Element 3.1 PC1, PC2

External test requirements

a *Recognise descriptions of the main components of the UK leisure and recreation industry, and identify examples of activities for each component.*

Range

Main components of the UK leisure and recreation industry: arts and entertainment, sports and physical activities, outdoor activities, heritage, play, catering and accommodation

Leisure and recreation activities: visits to arts centres, visits to entertainment centres, visits to heritage centres, sports participation, sports spectating, outdoor activities, playing, eating and drinking out

Arts and entertainment includes concerts, theatres, cinemas. Sports such as football, cricket, tennis and golf have people watching as well as taking part. Outdoor pursuits such as fishing, sailing, climbing, hiking and canoeing are enjoyed by many. Heritage centres, industrial museums and historic houses are interesting to visit. Playgrounds for children, areas to play games (such as golf and bowls) can be found in parks. Catering and accommodation can be from the simple to the elaborate, according to the type of tourist it is hoped to attract.

1 The arts and entertainment industries include:
   a multigym
   b catering exhibition
   c theatres
   d charity shops

2 An example of a heritage centre is the:
   a Tower of London
   b Bristol Zoo
   c Blackpool Tower
   d Sherwood Forest

3 A runner in the London Marathon would most likely be described as:
   a taking part in a sport
   b entertaining television viewers
   c taking part in an artificially-made attraction
   d advertising a sponsor

4 Eating and drinking out would most likely be described as:
   a an arts activity
   b a home-based activity
   c a leisure activity
   d a heritage activity

5 When two people decide to have a badminton match it is regarded as:
   a sports spectating
   b playing a game
   c multi-skilled sport
   d working-out with weights

6 An outdoor activity in which only children take part is:
   a golf
   b mountain climbing
   c a playground
   d water skiing

7 Sports spectating is a favourite leisure pursuit. Which two of the following sports are most likely to draw huge crowds of spectators in the UK?

1 rounders

2 bowling

3 football

4 cricket

Choose from:

a 1 and 2

b 2 and 3

c 3 and 4

d 1 and 4

External test requirements

b *Recognise descriptions of the main components of the UK travel and tourism industry, and identify examples of activities for each component.*

Range

Main components of the UK travel and tourism industry: travel services, incoming tours, outgoing tours, visitor attractions, information services, catering, accommodation, transport

Travel and tourism activities: travelling for pleasure, touring, going on holiday, visiting attractions, eating and drinking out.

Travel services can be obtained through organisers, tour operators, travel agents or by booking direct. Tour operators can take British tourists abroad, bring foreign tourists to the UK or organise tours of the UK for people who live there. Visitor attractions are often part of the UK tour and coach operators run day trips to a popular attraction. Information services include local guides, maps, brochures produced by the national tourist boards, leaflets, posters and TV advertisements. Catering varies from snack bars to high-class restaurants. Accommodation ranges from self-catering to luxury hotels. Tourists enjoy travelling for pleasure, taking an organised tour, going on holiday, visiting attractions and eating and drinking out.

8 Which of the following tourist activities is most likely to be found on the programme of an incoming tour to the UK?

a an adventure holiday for children

b a visit to Stratford-upon-Avon

c a camping weekend

d a visit to a garden centre

9 Which two of the following can be classed as offering catering to tourists?

1 picnic benches in a local park

2 a hot-dog seller

3 the Ritz hotel

4 drinks for the cyclists in the Tour de France

Choose from:

a 1 and 2

b 2 and 3

c 3 and 4

d 1 and 4

10 The *main* customers of Shearings Coach Tours are most likely to be:

a children going on a PGL holiday

b families being transported to the airport

c teenagers wanting an activity holiday

d the older age group

11 Tourists who want a reasonably-priced Sunday lunch with a drink afterwards would be most likely to choose:

a lunch at the Savoy

b sandwiches as they walk along

c a pub lunch

d a beefburger at McDonald's

Focus 2: Facilities, products and services

Reference: Element 3.1 PC3, PC4

External test requirements

a *Recognise descriptions and identify the facilities, products and services which make up the leisure and tourism industries in a given locality.*

Range

Leisure and recreation facilities: theatres, halls, tracks, museums, parks, sports centres, swimming pools, activity centres, heritage sites, play areas, catering provision, accommodation provision, natural environment features with leisure potential

Travel and tourist facilities: travel agencies, tour operators, principals, tourist information centres, tourist attractions, catering provision, accommodation provision

Main products and services: sports participation, sports spectating, outdoor activities, play, travel, catering, accommodation, entertainment, agency services, information services

Travel agents sell holidays to the public. Tour operators put the holidays together. The principals own travel organisations such as airlines, car-hire firms, ferry companies, shipping companies and railways. They may own their own travel agencies and hotels.

Tourist information centres have accommodation lists for visitors, as well as details of attractions, and information about local entertainment.

12 An example of a travel principal is:

a the head of a travel agency
b Aer Lingus
c the chief coach driver
d a mobile home

13 A tourist arriving in a strange town and wishing to find accommodation would ask the:

a local tour operator
b traffic warden
c tourist information centre
d sports hall

14 A package holiday would be put together by:

a a travel agency
b the local authority
c a car-hire firm
d a tour operator

Focus 3: Matching recreational needs to products and services

Reference: Element 3.1 PC5

External test requirements

a *Identify different recreational needs and match them to given products and services provided in a given locality.*

Range

Main products and services: sports participation, sports spectating, outdoor activities, play, travel, catering, accommodation, entertainment, agency services, information services

Needs: for physical activity, for social interaction, for a new experience, for a challenge, for personal satisfaction

People have different needs which are catered for by the leisure and tourism market, breaking customers down into types such as adults, families with children, business persons, people from the UK and from abroad. They all have different recreational needs which are catered for by different organisations in the industry.

15 A college student who wishes to look for a challenge would be most likely to take part in:
   a watching tennis on TV
   b the Duke of Edinburgh's Award Scheme
   c playing football with six-year-olds
   d making sandwiches to eat after roller-skating

16 Which of the following would children who thrive on physical activity be most likely to choose to meet their recreational needs?
   a quiz night at the local youth club
   b watching Dr Who videos
   c trying out painting by numbers pictures
   d joining the local swimming club

17 An older couple booking a holiday abroad and looking for a new experience would be most likely to ask a travel agent for information on:
   a white-water rapids in Canada using a canoe
   b sunny beaches in Majorca
   c a large impersonal hotel in Spain
   d a cruise in the Caribbean

18 Which of the following would best provide social interaction for an amateur cricket team?
   a drinks with supporters after the match
   b reading library books on how to improve bowling
   c arranging for the group to visit the theatre
   d writing an account of the match for the local paper

Investigate jobs in leisure and tourism

Leisure and tourism is now big business, with organisations putting their money into attractions and facilities all over the UK. These amenities all have to be managed, usually by a specialist business administrator. Business skills are needed to manage and develop tourism. Someone has to make policy decisions, work out long-term plans, give out the work, oversee the assistants and set the targets. This kind of work is found in bigger organisations, in big travel firms and large hotel groups, but it can also be found in local government. Smaller centres also need management skills. Generally employees reach the higher level jobs on offer after working their way up through the business, but if you are aiming at management you will need to take further qualifications at Intermediate and Advanced level and perhaps think about a degree in Business, Management Studies or Tourism.

Besides jobs such as a travel consultant in a travel shop, a reservations agent for a tour operator or a business travel agent, booking travel services for companies and the business traveller, there are back-up jobs. These are usually with the larger companies who need business administrators, accountants, computer specialists and secretaries.

People who work in leisure and tourism should have a pleasant personality, be presentable and have common sense. Most of the work is dealing with customers so they must communicate effectively face-to-face, by letter or by telephone. It is necessary to work as part of a team, to work closely with other people to achieve business objectives.

Qualifications

Skills and qualifications can be obtained at different levels. At Level I (Foundation level) the jobs will be a range of varied activities which are mainly routine. This level is equivalent to four GCSEs Grades D to G. The grade achieved depends on the final grade of the portfolio. There are NVQ (National Vocational Qualification) or SVQ (Scottish Vocational Qualification) and GNVQ (General National Vocational Qualification) or GSVQ (General Scottish Vocational Qualification) in Leisure and Tourism which are obtained at school or college.

The paths for school leavers to follow are as follows.

▶ **NVQ (National Vocational Qualification) or SVC (Scottish Vocational Qualification)** which is obtained in the workplace and assessed there, or by study in an Approved Centre linked with work experience. The skills are assessed on the job by a qualified assessor using a checklist of what is expected. The Level II is equivalent to GNVQ or GSVQ Intermediate level.
▶ **GNVQ (General National Vocational Qualification) or GSVQ (General Scottish Vocational Qualification) in Leisure and Tourism – Intermediate Level** which is done at school or college and is equivalent to four GCSEs Grades A–C or the Scottish equivalent.
▶ **NVQ/SVQ Level III** which is equivalent to GNVQ/GSVQ Advanced Level in Leisure and Tourism. This equals two Advanced level subjects of the General Certificate in Education.
▶ **NVQ/SVQ Level IV** is done at work with assessment through an Approved Centre and is equivalent to a degree course, e.g. a BA in Travel and Tourism.
▶ The final **NVQ/SVQ Level V**, when available, will be work-based and equivalent to a post-graduate qualification through a university or college of higher education, e.g. Master in Business Administration.

Universities and polytechnics will expect applicants to have GNVQ work at Merit or Distinction levels. Other routes to higher education are through the usual GCSEs Grades A–C and most places ask for Mathematics and English. They usually require two Advanced level subjects if people are offering academic rather than vocational qualifications.

Jobs in leisure and tourism

Some examples of jobs in the leisure and tourism industry are given in the next few pages. Although *your* particular ideal job may not be shown here, you will find something which you could do and use as a starting point to prepare for employment.

The majority of booking is now done through a computer terminal, so computer skills are very useful whatever other qualifications you may have. Sales and marketing experts are needed with imagination and persuasive skills to get the message across to the customer. Administration and accounting experts are needed to make sure that records are accurate and to give financial information to the management.

Many jobs have natural progression built in so that the beginner can see a career structure in front of him or her. Experience in the field is always valuable to have.

ACTIVITY 1

Work in small groups of 2 to 4 people.

1 Discuss jobs which you know about, have had experience of, or have observed being carried out in the following fields:

- entertainment
- sports
- outdoor activities
- heritage or history
- travel
- tourism
- catering services
- accommodation services
- travel agency services
- information services.

Suggest a job in each field which would be suitable for a beginner. If you think of more than one job, decide whether to include them all in the list.

2 Make a copy of the list for each member of the group.

CORE SKILL: *Communication 1.1 Take part in discussions*
PC 1, 2, 3, 4
Range: 1, 2, 3, 4.

Finding out about jobs

The careers office and the job centres are good places to start looking. The careers officer often has a list of part-time jobs suitable for students which could be a way in to a full-time career when you are qualified. Regional and national tourist boards will discuss plans with the local authority, and reports of these will appear in newspapers or on local radio. This may help students to make up their minds about the way they wish to go. There may be local associations of hotel keepers, restaurant owners and publicans which could give information about new projects.

The main source of job vacancies in the UK is through advertising. This can be done:

- in local newspapers
- outside the establishment on notice boards
- through the job centre
- from advertisements placed in school, college or the careers office by the careers officer
- in technical or professional trade journals and magazines.

There are also opportunities for finding out about job vacancies by letting family and friends know you are looking. Sometimes job agencies may find work for you in catering.

The leisure and tourism industries cover a wealth of jobs. To use the facilities, people must first get to know about them, so the first jobs featured here are those in Information Services.

ACTIVITY 2

1 Look through the following four jobs and match the person specification (the kind of person the employer is looking for) to your own qualities and characteristics. Find the job with the closest 'match'.

2 Discuss this as a job possibility with a fellow student and possibly your tutor.

Jobs in information

Tourist information centre assistant

Ginette works in the local tourist information centre. Although this is a large centre and she works as part of a team with a full-time job, she knows that in some smaller towns the work is seasonal. The centre is in the town hall, but it is going to be moved shortly to a small shop in the town centre shopping arcade.

Ginette can give advice on anything to do with the local area, as the team has created a database of useful information and travel facilities which is easy to call up to answer queries. These may come through face-to-face contact as customers come into the centre, through the post as queries which need a written answer, or via the telephone, so Ginette has to have good communication skills.

She has to handle cash and work the till, as the team sell booklets and postcards. They also hand out leaflets and give information on local and national attractions, and have created a display of information which people can browse through. Ginette also liaises with local hotels and guesthouses, and will book accommodation there for visitors on request.

Person specification:

▶ patience
▶ tact
▶ neat appearance
▶ good telephone manner
▶ a liking for meeting people
▶ the ability to operate a computer and a till
▶ good communication skills
▶ good local knowledge.

Qualifications:

▶ four GCSEs Grades C–E or GNVQ/GSVQ Foundation in Leisure and Tourism or Business.

Progression:

▶ similar work in a regional or national tourist board, progressing to supervisor or management positions.

Local authority tourism officer and assistant

Andrew is the local authority tourism officer and he is assisted by Ryan. Even if the area in which you live does not spring readily to mind as the best place to take a holiday, it may have many interesting features and amenities which visitors will enjoy. People come into the area on business, to see friends or relatives, on a day trip or need something to do in the long school holidays.

Andrew is part of the leisure and recreation team, although he knows that in larger authorities there are specialist staff working in different departments such as 'Advertising' or 'Heritage' with their own managers and teams. His job involves persuading potential investors to plan and develop tourist amenities in the area. New complexes will bring in other businesses to supply their needs. Visitors will arrive and spend their money, so this is an important part of the work.

Together with his assistant, Ryan, he writes local guides, has maps drawn and brochures or leaflets printed, negotiates advertising space so that the facilities become known. He works out special 'packages' for business conferences and manages exhibitions. Andrew has a Marketing degree and Ryan has GNVQ II in Leisure and Tourism, and is working on a day-release basis for GNVQ Level III. He hopes to become a tourism officer some day.

Person specification:

- able to keep an overview while checking details
- enthusiastic
- an extrovert
- able to negotiate
- a problem solver
- a good organiser
- able to write interesting promotions.

Qualifications:

- tourism officer – GNVQ/GSVQ Level III in Business or Leisure and Tourism, followed by a related degree in Business Administration, Marketing or Sales
- tourism assistant – GNVQ/GSVQ Level II in Business or Leisure and Tourism.

Progression:

- tourism officer – local authority planning officer, conference or marketing manager
- tourism assistant – local authority tourism officer.

Marketing officer/marketing assistant

Anna is the marketing officer and she is assisted by Shazad. Anna's job is to promote a service or product by creating a demand for it. She has to find ways of interesting visitors in her area and of making it stand out from other areas. Besides Shazad, Anna has a secretary, Joanne, and three clerical staff. These positions are sometimes used as a springboard to marketing assistant or even marketing officer jobs, when further qualifications have been taken, as the experience in the department is very useful. Anna has to be able to lead the team, and Shazad to work as part of it.

Selling the area may be done through advertising, brochures, trade fairs and exhibitions – anywhere in fact where special kinds of holidays or tours can be sold. Anna has turned a local water park into a big success through her marketing expertise, and she is now working on another plan for a large concert hall in the town centre. She is working with suppliers of different services and bringing them together, so that a package can be offered for visitors to the concert hall. Shazad is working on a tour of the area which will combine visits to heritage centres with visits to the factory shops in the area, with meals and accommodation provided as part of the tour.

Anna is also working on plans by the Regional Tourist Board to build a new sports arena in the town centre.

Person specification:

- imagination to see a potential service or product
- the ability to prepare promotions
- initiative to develop new projects
- the ability to analyse information
- a good memory for detail
- the ability to work under pressure
- good communication skills
- the ability to set targets for the team
- a talent for working with people
- the ability to create, plan, cost and implement projects.

Qualifications:

- marketing officer – Diploma or Degree in Business Administration, Management or Marketing and Sales
- marketing assistant – GNVQ/GSVQ Level II in Leisure and Tourism or Business.

Progression:

- marketing officer – higher managerial posts in regional or national tourist boards or businesses concerned with tourism
- marketing assistant – with experience and a related degree, a move into management in tourism recreation and leisure departments.

Tourist guide

Natalie is a self-employed tourist guide, but she has been

booked by a local tour operator to take coach loads of visitors from abroad round various heritage centres and historic sites in England. She meets the coach at the hotel, takes the visitors round the various attractions and has organised the tour so that she is dropped off at the bus station, to travel back to her own car while the visitors go on to their next hotel. She has researched all the attractions herself, looked at their history and architecture and worked out how to present the information in an interesting way. She weaves in some anecdotes, gossip and folk-tales which add to the enjoyment of the group. She answers the group's questions, if she can, and admits it if she can't! She has an authoritative manner and has worked out that when she needs the group to gather round and hear what she has to say, she will hold her arm up in the air as a signal – and also so that they can see her.

Natalie can speak French and works for a tour operator who brings in a tour of French people once a week. Natalie took a part-time training course run by her local authority before she decided to work as a tourist guide.

Adam is a Blue Badge tourist guide. He took early retirement from his job and decided to follow his interest in the history and architecture of his local town. He has taken training and obtained a qualification, which shows that he is top of the class where tourist guides are concerned. Like Natalie, he has done his own research and does freelance work, taking parties round the town centre and pointing out interesting features and places of historical significance.

Person specification:

- patience
- tact
- stamina
- good health
- wide knowledge of the locality
- the ability to speak to a group
- a lively personality
- general interest in the subject matter
- good organisational ability
- an authoritative manner
- possibly a foreign language
- an interest in history and architecture.

Qualifications:

- part-time training courses with high standards and rigorous examinations including presentation, history, social history,

architecture, buildings and places of interest, for Blue Badge
guides
▶ local authority training courses for tourists guides.

Progression:

▶ the experience would be useful for anyone starting their own
business in tour operations.

ACTIVITY 3

Work in pairs.

You will have noticed that many of the
qualities or characteristics in the information
handling side of leisure and tourism are similar
for various jobs.

1 Write down four of the jobs listed in
Activity 1 in this unit.

2 Think of related jobs which need the same
kinds of qualities. Write down at least one
related job for each of the jobs you have
chosen, e.g. tourist guide: tour
representative.

Jobs in accommodation services

These jobs may be part-time or full-time, depending on the size
of the establishments. Looking after people when they are away
from home calls for the same skills in a small establishment as
in a big hotel. It is all about making people feel welcome,
looking after their comfort and keeping up high standards.
Large hotels have clearly defined areas with different levels of
work, often with a recognised structure, so that employees can
work their way up the ladder. People work in teams, and the
teams work with each other. 'Reception' has to know which
rooms are available, and 'Housekeeping' needs to know how
many guests are expected. In a smaller establishment, there are
flexible job roles and if the owners also work in the business,
staff often like the 'family' feeling which comes from knowing
the employer personally. They may prefer this to working for a
large impersonal hotel group.

Chambermaid

The chambermaid is the person whose basic job is to do all the
domestic work, such as cleaning the rooms, making beds,
renewing stocks of items in the bedroom and bathroom,

replacing towels and leaving the rooms clean and tidy ready for the next guest.

There may be work to be done in other areas of the hotel. The public rooms must be dusted, carpets vacuumed, furniture cleaned and polished. The work may be done in shifts as guests move in and out at all hours.

Person specification:

- a responsible attitude
- the ability to operate cleaning equipment
- a good memory for detail
- a liking for working at a routine job
- stamina.

Qualifications:

- training is usually provided on the job, but people who have had domestic experience will find it useful.

Progression:

- housekeeper or supervisory positions in hotels, conference centres and hospitals.

Concierge or hall porter

David had worked his way up to maintenance foreman, when his firm decided to amalgamate two branches and close down the premises where he worked. After spending some weeks unemployed, he obtained a job as hall porter in a fairly large hotel in the town centre.

His supervisory experience was to prove useful as he was in charge of the junior porters, after receiving in-house training himself.

David is in charge of a team who receive guests from cars, coaches or taxis and carry in their luggage. He makes theatre bookings, takes messages, organises car rentals or taxis for the guests and makes sure that the team are working well.

Person specification:

- the ability to work out duty rotas
- a smart appearance
- friendliness
- the ability to deal with enquiries
- the ability to deal with complaints
- an interest in the local area
- knowledge of entertainments

- a liking for people
- the ability to supervise junior staff.

Qualifications:

- a general reception course would give suitable qualifications, or a move from another supervisory role would be useful.

Progression:

- this could be to other positions within the hotel, but would probably need some formal qualifications; a part-time General Reception Course may lead to a move to reception work.

Housekeeper

Most housekeepers are women, and Julie joined the hotel staff at 16 as assistant housekeeper. Four years later, she has moved into the housekeeper's job.

Julie makes sure that all the domestic work is done efficiently, on time and within the budget she is allowed. She supervises the domestic staff, makes sure that rooms are thoroughly cleaned, beds made, and stocks of bedroom hot drinks and bathroom toiletries are in place. It is a very demanding job and sometimes Julie is needed in her off-duty hours, so she lives on the premises. She checks that the public rooms are also ready for visitors, that flower arrangements are in place, and works out the rotas for part-time staff who are on her team. She also liaises with Reception who inform her of accommodation required.

Person specification:

- a good appearance
- an eye for detail
- good communication skills
- the ability to organise and supervise other people
- a responsible attitude
- the ability to design rooms and choose the decoration
- the ability to do simple accounts.

Qualifications:

- the City & Guilds Housekeeping course covers the basics and is a useful qualification, or training can be on the job.

Progression:

- supervisory or managerial positions in hotels, leisure centres, educational institutions, hospitals, holiday centres or banqueting and conference rooms; the experience is also useful to anyone thinking of moving on to owning or managing a small hotel.

Jobs in catering

The chef

Paul is in charge of the kitchen in a banqueting suite and frequently has several different functions requiring several different meals to cater for at the same time.

He has trained in different establishments and worked in different branches of cooking. He plans the menus, makes sure that stocks of ingredients are in hand and that his team all know what to do. When he worked in a much smaller establishment, Paul did some of the preparation and cooking himself, but now he takes on a chiefly supervisory role. He has commis and sous chefs working under him and co-ordinates the work, so that the different meals required at different times are ready when they are needed.

Person specification:

- patience
- the ability to delegate
- imagination in preparing and cooking food
- the ability to supervise a team
- stamina
- understanding of nutrition
- the ability to produce a balanced menu
- willingness to experiment.

Qualifications:

- training as a chef can be undertaken through a college course working towards City & Guilds and then about three years working through all the sections of a large kitchen and each area of food preparation as a commis and sous chef.

Progression:

- top chefs may move to international hotels, banqueting or conference centres where high quality cuisine is required.

Catering assistant

Leroy is a student who has found a part-time job in the evenings and at weekends as a counter assistant in a branch of a well-known fast food establishment. The branch has rather a high staff turnover rate as the pay isn't very high and the work can be tiring. In Leroy's case, the food has to be cooked and served quickly, as customers are in a hurry and he needs to turn out beefburgers on a bun, chips, chicken nuggets, pasta and serve cold drinks as well. The customers wait at the counter for the food and then take it away themselves. Leroy also has to take money, operate the till and give change in between cooking. He has also worked for a firm where he had to use a fryer and a microwave oven. At the close of the day, Leroy cleans the equipment and the counter while other staff make the customer areas fit for the next session.

Person specification:

- the ability to work in a team
- neat clean appearance
- the ability to operate the equipment
- a good memory for orders
- efficiency
- a liking for working at a routine job
- friendly manner.

Qualifications:

- training is usually on the job, but employees may benefit from a college catering course.

Progression:

- managing a fast food establishment or buying and operating a franchise. (This is where the operator pays an initial licensing fee plus a share of the profits to the organisation giving the franchise for the use of the trade name and the security and expertise of a large organisation behind them. The harder the individual operator works, the more profit he or she makes.) Examples of fast food franchises are Kentucky Fried Chicken and Pizza Hut. A franchise has a much lower rate of failure than other owner-managed businesses.

Bar staff

When Scott reached the age of 18, he decided to supplement his student income by applying for a job in a bar. The job consisted of rather more than just pouring drinks. Before the doors opened, Scott had to get the bar ready for customers; checking the glasses, putting out the nuts and the clean ashtrays, and chalking up the day's Pub Grub menu. Many pubs now offer snacks and bar staff are expected to serve food as well as drink. Scott also had to take away empty glasses and plates, wipe up spills and tidy up at the end of the session.

He had to remember the various drinks and know their prices, know who was next to be served, take the money, enter the various items and give the receipt and the change. He had to remember to give special attention to the regulars and give friendly attention to everyone.

Scott only worked in the evenings on Thursdays, Fridays and Saturdays which were the busiest times, but when the local team (which had a football ground near the bar) was playing at home, Scott also worked during the middle of the day on Saturdays. He found the hours unsocial and realised that this could be the reason for the high turnover in bar staff and the availability of jobs.

Person specification:

- be able to remember several items in an order
- have a pleasant personality
- be able to remember the prices of a range of drinks
- realise that regulars should be given special attention (perhaps addressed by name)
- be able to serve food and coffee
- know how to operate a till
- be able to work under pressure.

Qualifications:

- you may learn bar skills as part of a catering course at college or be trained by the establishment offering you a job.

Progression:

- supervisory or managerial positions in a large hotel or bar; tenant or owner of a public house.

Useful addresses for finding out more information about this section are:

Hotel, Catering & Institutional Management Association
191 Trinity Road
LONDON   SW17 7HN

Hotel & Catering Training Board Careers Department
International House
High Street
Ealing
LONDON   W5 5DB

Look back at the information you have just read about jobs in accommodation or catering services. Choose a job which you would like to do part-time or as work experience and write a short account of how this job would fit in with your:

- present circumstances
- present qualifications or qualifications you are now trying to obtain
- interests
- skills
- personality.

CORE SKILL: *Communication 1.2 Produce written material*
PC 1, 2, 3, 4
Range 1, 2, 3 (outline), 4

Jobs in travel

The baggage and freight handler

When holiday-makers check in at the airport, their baggage moves on a conveyor belt and they do not see it again until they reach their destination.

Mike is a baggage and freight handler at his local airport. He works shifts which are given to him a week in advance and which cover seven days a week. Some baggage handlers work during the night to move freight and mail, but Mike has a temporary job which lasts from April to October (when there are more people using the airport to go on holiday).

He works as part of a team handling the baggage and loading it on to planes going all over the world. Mike keeps his eyes open and checks the labels on the luggage to make sure that suitcases are going to the correct place. He has to work quickly once the team moves into action, as there is not a lot of time to unload the plane and get it ready for the return journey. There are no regular meal breaks – the team will have a snack when they are not loading a plane.

When Mike returns the luggage trolleys to the reception area of the airport he is often asked for information and directions. Part of his job is to take wheelchair users to the plane and to take them on board before the other passengers embark, so he has to be sensitive to their needs.

Person specification:

- tact

- patience
- good communication skills
- the ability to work under pressure
- stamina
- good teamwork skills
- the ability to lift and handle baggage and freight.

Qualifications:

- no qualifications are necessary for general baggage handling, but a clean driving licence is needed for driving trucks in the airport.

Progression:

- supervisor or foreperson
- duty manager for baggage and freight handling services.

Air cabin crew

Shabana wanted to be an air stewardess during her last two years at school. After working for a GNVQ Foundation in Leisure and Tourism, she wrote off to all the airlines she could find in *Yellow Pages* to ask for a job. She was asked to go for an interview for a temporary contract during the summer months. After tests and interviews, she was accepted on the understanding that when the airline required her, they would telephone and she would respond. She went on the airline's own training scheme which covered galley management, food services, first-aid and emergency procedures and then went home to wait for her first telephone call.

On her first flight, there was a senior steward in charge of the team which Shabana had joined. Her job was to show passengers to their seats, check that they were fastened in before take-off and help them to put hand luggage away. Once in the air, she helped to serve drinks, duty-free goods and gave out the meal. As this was a European trip, the cabin crew were active for the whole time, but Shabana knew that on a long trip she would be handing out pillows and blankets and be able to spend some time watching the in-flight movie.

Shabana found that there were strict rules about the length of duties. On the return trip, the aircraft was two hours later than scheduled so it missed out a landing at Heathrow. The passengers had to be taken back by coach from Manchester. Shabana was pleased to find that she didn't need to call on her first-aid and emergency procedures on her first trip!

Person specification:

- at least 20 years of age
- at least 1.65m in height
- able to keep calm in a crisis
- able to swim
- in good health
- able to cope with giving change in different currencies
- of good appearance
- able to cope with time-zone changes
- good at looking after people
- knowledgeable about first-aid and emergency procedures.

Qualifications:

- at least four GCSEs Grades A–C including if possible a language
- nursing or catering experience is useful
- ability to complete the Airline Training Scheme to a satisfactory standard.

Progression:

- senior steward or stewardess
- supervisory or management positions in hotels, conference or banqueting centres.

Coach driver

Winston has always been interested in cars and driving. He worked in a garage as a trainee mechanic for three years after he left school and then took a PSV (Public Service Vehicle) licence. When he reached the age of 21 he was eligible to drive larger vehicles such as coaches, and decided to look for a job with a coach firm.

He now works for a travel firm specialising in coach holidays. Sometimes he takes a coach to the Continent and has to understand the use of a tachograph, which records the distances and rest breaks for the driver when abroad. More often he drives in the UK, where it is up to the driver to keep to the organisation's rules about rest breaks so that driving is safe.

Winston reads maps and works his routes out, plans the stops for snacks and lunch and decides where he will be able to park. When he takes a coach party on tour, he stays with them and takes them out on excursions during their holiday.

He finds his garage experience useful, as he is able to carry out basic repairs in an emergency.

Person specification:

- excellent driving skills
- the ability to map read and work out routes
- good health
- some mechanical knowledge
- the ability to keep to a schedule
- sensitivity to passengers' needs
- the ability to load and unload luggage.

Qualifications:

- PSV licence and experience in driving; City & Guilds offer courses in the mechanics of vehicle maintenance.

Progression:

- managing the organisation of a coach operation.

Tour operations manager

There are different sizes of tour operators, though the market has become dominated by four or five large groups. There are still small operators, especially those who offer specialist holidays or domestic tour operators running coach holidays in the UK.

Robert works for a small firm offering holidays in Portugal, both on the Algarve and in the north of Portugal. He knows that although large firms have different departments for marketing, writing the brochures, looking at new locations and future possibilities, he will have to do all this himself.

The first thing he has to do is to decide the venue for the package holiday and see what it offers for the tourist. Accommodation and meals are worked out, flights from the UK decided upon, attractions located and the timings worked out. Next, the whole thing must be costed, overheads added and the profits calculated. Descriptions, photographs, the itinerary, dates, times and prices are put together in a brochure which is sent out to travel agents who will book the clients.

Person specification:

- the ability to plan itineraries
- the ability to negotiate prices
- interest in specialist areas
- the ability to visualise development opportunities
- good organisational skills
- the ability to draw up budgets
- familiarity with legal requirements

- the ability to market the product
- good promotional material-writing skills.

Qualifications:

- ABTA offer The Certificate of Tour Operating Practice and The Certificate of Tour Operating Management. GNVQ modules in Business or Leisure and Tourism are useful.

Progression:

- this is useful experience for running your own business providing tours.

Addresses for more information about these jobs:

British Airways Recruitment Section
PO Box 10
Heathrow Airport
Hounslow
LONDON   TW6 2JA

Careers and Occupational Information Centre
Moorfoot
SHEFFIELD   S1 48Q
(Pilots and Cabin Crew)
(Working in Travel)

ABTA National Training Board
Waterloo House
11–17 Chertsey Road
WOKING
Surrey   GU21 5AL

ACTIVITY 5

Some of the jobs under the heading 'travel' may not be suitable for you as a school or college leaver, but would be possible as you gain more qualifications.

1 Choose a job from this section, or from another section if you prefer, which you might like to apply for some time in the future. Write down the main tasks and responsibilities for the job you have chosen.

2 Write a short paragraph about yourself, your personality, skills, interests and qualifications which you think would make you suitable for this type of job when you have obtained more qualifications.

Jobs in sport

Leisure centre receptionist

Jane saw an advertisement for this job in her local paper and
applied at once. She wanted a job which fitted in with her
domestic life and looking after two school-age children. The job
was shared with two other people on a three-week rota, and
covered every night of the week and all day Saturday and
Sunday. Jane worked one Saturday in three, and either Sunday
morning for six hours, or Sunday afternoon and evening for six
hours, with the next Sunday off. This fitted in well with taking
the children to and from school and meant that school holidays
were no problem.

Jane answers telephone enquiries, books out the different
facilities, deals with queries, handles the cash and sells drinks
and snacks which are on offer at the reception desk.

Several customers arrive together and Jane has to deal with
them all quickly. She offers information about the courses on
offer, puts people in touch with the specialist coach and gives
help and advice if necessary.

Lyndsey is a student who needs to boost her income. She works
in the local sports centre issuing tickets for the swimming pool
and other facilities. The work is part-time and on a rota. When
she begins a session, there is a 'float' of money and a number of
tickets. At the end of the session, the money should equal the
number of tickets sold plus the 'float'. This kind of job may also
take place in a theme park where the ticket clerk issues tickets
for the rides and may have to explain safety factors to the
customers. In some cases, the ticket clerk is the first to spot
trouble or people needing help.

These two jobs call for a similar person specification.

Person specification:

▸ be able to issue tickets
▸ be able to book facilities
▸ be able to add up accurately
▸ take cash and give change
▸ have a friendly personality
▸ give information
▸ be able to operate a till and possibly a computer terminal
▸ be calm and tactful
▸ be a good communicator, both face-to-face and on the
  telephone.

Qualifications:

▶ GCSE Mathematics Grade A–C or, if mature, evidence of experience in handling money.

Progression:

▶ travel agency or tour operations work
▶ tour guide.

Leisure centre assistant

A multi-sports leisure centre will have facilities for squash, trampolining, badminton, indoor tennis, five-a-side football, keep fit, dance, judo and softball. There will probably be outdoor pitches which can be booked for cricket and football.

Aftab is a keen cricket player and works full-time as a leisure centre assistant. He hopes to coach cricket in the near future. At the moment his work involves putting up nets, getting equipment ready and putting it all away at the end of the session. If youngsters are using the facilities, Aftab will keep a supervisory eye on them.

When Aftab qualifies as a cricket coach, he will join the other specialist coaches who work with individuals or groups of people showing them how to improve their sporting skills and the best way of doing things. This may involve giving instructions, or actually playing the game with the learner.

Neil works at the swimming pool as he is a strong swimmer with a life-saving certificate. His duties include supervising the swimmers and looking after the poolside and changing rooms.

Both jobs need similar person specifications.

Person specification:

▶ a general interest in sport
▶ the ability to coach in specialist subjects
▶ stamina
▶ the ability to get on well with people
▶ knowledge of first-aid and perhaps life-saving techniques
▶ the ability to supervise and a firm manner
▶ a responsible attitude
▶ physical fitness.

Qualifications:

▶ GNVQ/GSVQ Level II in Leisure and Tourism, a life-saving certificate, special coaching qualifications from a Sports Association and skill in the specialist sport offered.

Progression:

- business and entertainment management, with some related advanced qualification.

Technician

Theme parks and museums have machinery which must be operated safely and engineers and technicians have the responsibility to see that this happens.

Craig has a Diploma in Electronic Engineering and has chosen to work in a theme park. If the roller-coaster needs repairing, it is his job to put it right. In the winter, he strips down and services all the rides, and checks any new ones which have been put in. He must know how they work so that he can take care of any faults and problems.

He also helps to build and maintain the machinery for the special effects, and looks after the models. Occasionally he has to restore or preserve some of the exhibits in the theme park.

Person specification:

- mechanical aptitude
- the ability to work with diagrams and drawings
- reliability and accuracy
- the ability to deal with customers
- good knowledge of the machinery used
- the ability to assess faults and make repairs.

Qualifications:

- Certificate or Diploma in Engineering or Electronics, possibly combined with training on the job or experience in operating equipment.

Progression:

- design work
- supervisor.

The Careers and Occupational Information Centre has information about careers in physical education and sport.

Work in pairs.

1 Choose one of the jobs in the 'Jobs in sport' section.

2 Design a questionnaire to find out the advantages and disadvantages of the chosen job, using a word processor for the finished product.

3 Take some copies and each visit a different sports facility. Ask as many people as possible who work there to answer the questions for you. This means that you interview them, not leave them a piece of paper to fill in!

4 When you and your partner have completed your questionnaires, go through them together to discover:

- advantages
- disadvantages
- whether work is done by: part-timers, full-timers, permanent or temporary staff
- hours of work averaged over a week
- how they came to know about the job
- who they report to
- who reports to them.

Jobs in history and heritage

People who visit the UK find that historic sites, houses and other buildings (such as heritage museums) are fascinating. They are also drawn to art galleries, theatres and concert halls, as well as to the natural beauties of national parks and other scenic areas. As all these attractions are quite conveniently situated, from the jobs' point of view, all round the country, there is work in most regions.

Museum curator

Lauren was a good all-rounder at school and could not decide at first what degree to take when she went to university. Eventually she decided on Archaeology and obtained a good degree. Her first post was in a small museum, but now she is the curator of a much larger establishment in one of the major cities. She has staff to help her as she cleans and catalogues exhibits, prepares educational materials, and catalogues and decides on the purchase of new exhibits.

From time to time, Lauren designs special exhibitions, using the museum's own collection of objects and borrowing from other sources. The exhibits have to be interpreted for the public, so that they understand them when they come to view and she is also responsible for this and for administration. Lauren needs to be accurate, dedicated, committed and able to work with a team.

Museum assistant

Rizwan went on a short course run by The Museums Association for museum attendants, which includes security. He helps to look after the property and is especially alert at special exhibition times when there may be objects on loan from other places.

He also helps with the work of labelling, cleaning and mending, and then displaying the objects in the collection, and can deal with enquiries from visitors. He has also trained in emergency procedures and fire drill and understands the safety regulations.

Person specification:

- responsible attitude
- the ability to move large artifacts properly
- smart appearance
- the ability to deal with enquiries from the general public
- knowledge of safety and security procedures.

Qualifications:

- curator – First or Higher degree in a subject such as Art, History, Archaeology or the sciences; The Museums Association offer a post-graduate diploma
- assistant/attendant – four GCSEs Grades A–C and possibly some work experience obtained on a voluntary basis.

Progression:

- curator – promotion in own subject specialisation by moving to other institutions
- assistant/attendant – move into local authority amenity supervision.

Ticket issuing clerk

When people visit a museum, historic house or heritage centre they obtain a ticket which gives them entry. The ticket issuing clerk has a till with a 'float' – a certain sum of money to begin with so that change can be given. The first job is to check and count the money in the float, and if the till is being taken over from someone else, to check the money with that person.

Besides issuing tickets and giving the correct change, people may want to ask questions, buy leaflets or obtain information about the amenity so the clerk has to know all the basic facts. The clerk may have to alert staff if there is a school group which needs a guide or a disabled person who would appreciate some help.

At the end of the day, the clerk has to cash up and balance the till which should tally with the number of tickets sold and the money in the 'float'.

Person specification:

- be able to add up quickly
- know how to work a till and cash up
- have a pleasant manner
- be tidy in appearance
- have good communication skills
- have knowledge of the amenity
- be honest.

Qualifications:

- GCSE in Mathematics or a qualification in numeracy is useful
- experience in handling money, such as a part-time job in retailing is also helpful.

Progression:

- receptionist
- tour operations assistant
- supervisor in the retail trade.

Careers information

Your local careers office will have information on courses available for careers in leisure and tourism, and lists of colleges of further education and approved training centres suitable for those at school leaving age and for other entrants.

Your careers teacher and staff in job centres and specialist employment agencies will also be able to give you information about obtaining skills and qualifications. Remember that NVQs are obtained on the job and an assessor will certify your competence in the workplace. GNVQs can be full-time study with work experience, or full-time work with part-time studies. Obtaining a Level IV NVQ is the equivalent of a degree course and is done at work with part-time study.

There are opportunities for finding out about jobs from asking family or friends or people who work in the branch of leisure and tourism which you would like. Newspaper and magazine advertisements carry quite a lot of information about the jobs which they advertise, you can look at these to see what is usually required.

ACTIVITY 7

Work in pairs.

1 Through the sources listed above, or any other sources you can think of, obtain an advertisement for a job vacancy in a leisure or tourism organisation and cut it out. Each partner can choose a job vacancy each.

2 Imagine that the job advertisement asks you to telephone for an application form. When you do this, a voice says:

'There is no-one here just now to talk to you. Please leave your name and number and any message after the tone.' (This is followed by a 'ping' which you know is the tone.)

Compose a suitable message to leave for both your job vacancies.

Remember that the organisation may have several job advertisements in different places (newspapers, job centres, the careers

office) and will require details of the job for which you need the application form.

Don't forget to give your address!

3 When you are satisfied with your messages, have them recorded. If this is not possible, dictate the messages to each other.

4 You are now going to be the person in the organisation who is dealing with the recorded messages.

You will need to send out application forms to the people who have left messages, so address an envelope to the person who left the message, and in the top left-hand corner put two or three words to identify the job, for example: 'Receptionist/Sports centre' or 'Fast food chef'. Check with your partner that all the correct details have been given to enable you to carry out your task.

Careers advisers and officers from your local careers office can give much help and advice on careers in leisure and tourism, together with examples of job descriptions and person specifications for various kinds of work.

If your careers office has a computerised 'matching' system, you can feed in information about your skills, qualifications and preferences and be given a list of jobs which will fit in with these, which is quite a useful way to start looking at jobs.

You may wish to send off for reference materials and books about jobs in leisure and tourism to:

Careers and Occupational Information Centre
Moorfoot
SHEFFIELD
S1 4PQ

Careers in sport and recreation from:

The Physical Association
162 Kings Cross Road
LONDON
WC1X 9DH

Careers in leisure and recreation from:

Central Services for University and Polytechnic Careers Service
Crawford House
Precinct Centre
MANCHESTER
M13 9EP

The national tourist boards will also have information about setting up small businesses in leisure and tourism.

You may also research information from environmental and conservation organisations in your own locality whose addresses are in *Yellow Pages* or the *Thomson* directory.

Check your college, school or local library for careers books.

People who already work in the leisure and tourism field in which you are interested may be able to give you help, advice and information about careers in their organisation.

Evidence indicator

Gender and the place where you live are features in obtaining jobs in the leisure and tourism industries. Some people (e.g. women with domestic responsibilities or students) are looking for part-time work which will suit their circumstances.

1 Make notes on the range of job opportunities available in your own locality (the area in which you could travel to work from your home in about an hour). Give examples of at least five jobs which would suit a leisure and tourism student (not necessarily yourself):

a in the leisure and recreation industry.

b in the travel and tourism industry.

2 Look at two jobs which would suit you in *either* the leisure and recreation industry *or* travel and tourism. The first job should be suitable for your first employment and the second for further progression. Outline each job and include:

- ▶ why the job would be suitable for you
- ▶ the main purpose of the job
- ▶ what skills and qualifications are required to do the job
- ▶ how you personally would obtain the necessary skills and qualifications
- ▶ where you obtained the advice and information which you used for your outline.

Evaluation

When you have completed your **Evidence indicator**, look back at your plan of action, the sources you used and the information you obtained.

Decide which ideas were good ones and which could have been improved upon. Look at the alternatives you considered and say why you used the ones you chose instead of other ways of doing the job.

Revision and specimen test questions

Focus 4: Jobs

Reference: Element 3.2 PC1, PC2

External test requirements

a *Recognise descriptions of and identify the range of job opportunities in the leisure and tourism industries.*

Range

Range of job opportunities: in different components of the leisure and recreation industry, in different components of the travel and tourism industry

Jobs in leisure and recreation may be managing an amenity as a specialist business administrator, managing the local authority's leisure provision, making policy decisions, setting long-term targets and plans, and need good qualifications such as a degree in Business, Management Studies or Leisure and Tourism. There are also customer-related jobs directly providing the service, and support staff such as accountants, computer operators, administrators and secretaries.

1 Which one of the following best describes a person who writes guides to a local area, arranges for the printing of maps, brochures and leaflets, arranges for advertising of local conference and exhibition facilities in a local area or region?
   a travel agent
   b coach tour operator
   c historic house guide
   d local authority leisure and tourism manager

2 The job of looking after guest rooms and public rooms in a hotel would be done by a:
   a conference organiser
   b chambermaid
   c hall porter
   d marketing assistant

3 A part-time job cooking and serving beefburgers on a bun, chips, chicken nuggets and pasta is known as a:
   a chef
   b bar person
   c catering assistant
   d waiter

4 A job in a team which puts travellers' luggage on the correct aeroplane, gives information to passengers and helps wheelchair users at an airport is known as:
   a air cabin crew
   b steward
   c fork-lift trucker
   d baggage handler

5 A part-time job in which someone works at weekends and evenings answering telephone enquiries, taking bookings, handling cash and selling drinks and snacks is known as a:
   a swimming pool attendant
   b sports clerk
   c leisure centre receptionist
   d technician

External test requirements

b *Using the criteria for suitability of jobs, match jobs in leisure and tourism to given applicants.*

Range

Suitable: as initial employment, for progression in the industry; suited to the student's circumstances, suited to the student's interests

Some jobs in leisure and tourism do not need qualifications and training is given on the job. These jobs are suitable for initial employment, but if an employee wishes to progress then qualifications are useful. GNVQ/NVQ Level I (Foundation) is equivalent to four GCSEs Grades D–G. Level II is equal to four GCSEs Grades A–C, Level III is equivalent to two 'A' levels and NVQ Level IV is equivalent to a degree course. Employers who interview job applicants hope they will be suitable and remain in the job: a person whose qualifications are too high would probably want to leave as soon as a better opportunity came along.

6 A job as a tourist information centre assistant is advertised as needing someone who can give advice on the local area, handle cash, use a till, create displays of literature and match accommodation to the requirements of guests. This job would be suitable for someone with:
   a four GCSEs Grades D–G or GNVQ Foundation in Leisure and Tourism

b a Business degree

c a Higher Diploma in Art and Design

d NVQ Level IV

7 A job as head hall porter in a large hotel is advertised. Training can be offered to a suitable candidate, who should have supervisory experience or a general reception qualification.

Which one of the following applicants would most likely be called for interview?

a Wayne, a student leaving college in the middle of the course

b Stephen, a former maintenance foreman

c Daniel, a school leaver looking for his first job

d Mark, a graduate looking for temporary work

8 Arnold's Coach Company Ltd is looking for someone in their firm to progress to the position of managing a coach tour operation. Which one of the following would they be most likely to promote?

a the ticket issuing clerk

b a coach driver with ten years' experience

c the new trainee accountant

d a part-time receptionist

Focus 5: Purposes, skills and qualifications

Reference: Element 3.2 PC3, PC4, PC5

External test requirements

a *Recognise the main purposes of given jobs.*

Range

Main purposes: tasks, responsibilities

The main tasks and responsibilities of management jobs are to make plans for the future, to set targets and make sure they are carried out and to look at long-term prospects and how the money they need will be raised.

Supervisors will ensure that their team understand and can meet their targets, and will look at training needs.

Employees will make sure they work to the terms of their contract and keep to any measures introduced by the employers to ensure the health and safety of themselves, other people and the customers.

9 Which two of the following tasks would be the responsibility of a marketing officer in a local authority?

1 inspecting city centre shops

2 renting stalls in the local market

3 promoting the concert hall by creating a demand for it

4 advertising the area at exhibitions and trade fairs

Choose from:

a 1 and 2

b 2 and 3

c 3 and 4

d 1 and 4

10 Putting together a holiday package with travel, accommodation, meals and visits to places of interest would most likely be done by:

a a holiday guide

b a leisure assistant

c a tour operator

d a sales representative

11 Which of the following would a leisure centre assistant be most likely to have as a main responsibility?

a getting equipment ready and putting it away

b taking telephone bookings

c training the football team

d writing advertisements for new courses

12 A leisure and recreation department in a local authority aims to increase the number of visitors to the area from abroad by 10% during the next year. This target is most likely to be set by:
a the computer operator
b the administration officer's secretary
c the finance department
d the marketing manager

External test requirements

b *Identify the main skills and qualifications required for given jobs.*
c *Recognise appropriate sources of advice and information about given jobs, skills, and qualifications.*

Range

Skills: vocational skills, core skills

Qualifications: vocational, academic

Advice and information: on the purposes of jobs, on tasks and responsibilities of jobs, on skills and qualifications for jobs, on suitability of jobs

Appropriate sources: careers advisers, reference materials, other informed sources

Skills can be obtained at different levels and can be GNVQ/SNVQ Levels I to II or NVQ/SVQ Levels I to IV. To these should be added the core skills of Communication, Application of Number and Information Technology. Academic skills are GCSEs and Advanced Level certificates.

Advice and information can be obtained from careers advisers, reference materials (such as booklets explaining courses and qualifications) from other sources such as tutors or people working in the industry.

13 Which one of the following qualifications would a tourist guide in a historic city be most likely to possess?
a a degree in Art History
b training course certificate for Tourist Guides
c Duke of Edinburgh's Gold Award
d GNVQ Level I (Foundation) in Business

14 Which one of the following would most likely be a necessary qualification for a museum curator?
a a degree in Business Management
b four GCSEs Grades A–C
c GNVQ Level I in Leisure and Tourism
d degree in Archaeology

15 Which one of the following would be most likely to help a student who is not sure what jobs in leisure and tourism to find out about?
a a careers adviser
b a librarian
c a newspaper telesales section
d a National Tourist Board official

16 A student has completed a GNVQ Foundation Level in Leisure and Tourism and wishes to know the next qualification to aim for.

Which one of the following would be most likely to have the correct information and advice for the student:
a the local job centre
b a recreation and leisure assistant
c a college/school tutor
d the college/school first-aider

17 Which one of the following would be most likely to have information about careers in leisure and recreation after graduation?
a Airline cabin crew brochure
b 'Run Your Own Guesthouse' booklet
c Skills for Conservation booklet
d Management Careers in Leisure and Recreation booklet

Plan for employment in leisure and tourism

Personal information

Leisure and tourism is such a vast field that anyone looking for work will find that there are a number of different possibilities. Besides the jobs we see being done in leisure and tourism, there are the support services: the administration in the offices, secretarial and clerical work – these are all in the leisure and tourism sector.

Broad headings under which jobs can be classified are:

- **information and promotion** including: tourist information centre assistant, local authority tourism manager, guides: blue badge and historical costume, press officer, secretarial, telesales and clerical staff
- **travel and transport** including: travel agency assistant, coach company booking clerk, coach driver, air cabin crew, car-hire clerk, railway station workers, tour operations manager, holiday tour courier, sales and ticket booking staff
- **accommodation** including: hotel manager, receptionist, hall porter, housekeeper, security staff, cleaning staff, administration staff
- **catering** including: fast food cook, chef, waiter or waitress, counter assistant, bar staff, manager, kitchen staff, pub tenants/owners
- **sport and leisure** including: management staff, leisure centre assistant, specialist coach, sales staff, receptionist, ticket issuing clerk, sports equipment rental assistant, equipment/facilities technician
- **heritage and conservation** including: historic house manager, museum curator, assistant curator (specialist subjects), souvenir shop assistant, conservation worker, warden, heritage centre manager, nature reserve manager
- **theatres, cinemas, TV studios** including: ticket issuing

clerks, snacks, fast food and bar staff, technicians, stage staff, support staff (administration, cleaning services, security).

The local authority will employ many people in their leisure services department. Jobs in libraries, swimming pools, sports centres and sports fields, museums and art galleries will all come under the local authority.

ACTIVITY 1

Work in small groups or in pairs.

1 Choose from the following personal features those which are closest to your own and write them down:

a ▶ likes to work with people
▶ likes to work alone
▶ is happy to do either

b ▶ likes to talk to people
▶ does not like to speak to strangers (customers)
▶ would speak to customers if training was given first

c ▶ likes to lead a group or team
▶ likes to be a member of a group or team and discuss what to do
▶ likes to be told what to do

d ▶ likes to do the same work every day
▶ likes to do different work every day
▶ is happy to do either

e ▶ likes to learn how to do new things
▶ does not like change
▶ does not like learning new things

f ▶ is happy to keep in the same job
▶ would like to progress in the job
▶ would like to take more qualifications

2 When you have finished, discuss your answers to question 1 with the group, to see if they agree with you.

3 Look at the broad headings and jobs given at the beginning of this chapter and write down:

a jobs which you think you could do now.
b jobs which you might do with experience and training in future.
c jobs which you do not think are suited to you.

Gender and the place where you live are often factors in getting jobs. For example, women who have families to look after often prefer part-time jobs, because these will fit in with their lifestyle.

Jobs in leisure often ask for people to work when other people are free, e.g. during the evening or at weekends. Transport must be thought about as it may not be easy to get to a place of work when there is less public transport to travel on. You may widen the range of jobs for which you can apply once you are able to drive and have a car.

Personal qualities

Besides the personal features or characteristics which you have worked on in the last activity, the employer may be interested to know if you:

▶ have neat handwriting
▶ are reliable
▶ are punctual
▶ can speak clearly
▶ sound friendly and interested
▶ are polite
▶ have a positive outlook
▶ are a willing worker and do not grumble
▶ dress suitably
▶ will undertake more training, perhaps in your own time.

You may be able to include these qualities on an application form.

Are you right for the job?

When you have thought about the jobs which you would like to do, you then have to consider whether *you* are the right person for the job.

You may be asked if you have any **aptitudes** (this is a natural ability for doing something such as playing team games, swimming or aerobics). You may be asked if you have **manual dexterity**. 'Manual' means doing something with your hands and 'dexterity' is the quality of being skilful. Have you got nimble fingers? Can you put parts of machinery together or assemble equipment to be used for leisure activities, such as a trampoline?

Physique is important for some leisure jobs. If you want to be a member of the air cabin crew, you have to be at least 5'4" tall so that you can reach the overhead lockers.

Your job may need someone who is fit and healthy – it is difficult to coach a sport if you cannot run! Some jobs in leisure require **stamina** which is the ability to keep going without getting too tired to work and this is something which you may be asked about.

Your appearance will probably matter to your employer. He or she is not likely to be looking for Miss World or Mr Universe – just a neat and tidy person who could fit into the organisation without causing the customers to be put off the leisure pursuit for ever!

If you have already had a part-time job in leisure or been a keen follower of the kind of activity in which you want employment, this is usually a point in your favour. You will already know that as an employee you are expected to be prompt and reliable, pleasant and polite, and you may be able to use a part-time work experience employer as a referee. Remember that you should always ask someone before you give his or her name and address as a referee.

You should also think about where you might progress from your initial job. Many organisations have training courses which employees can undertake, often in the firm's own time, which will give further qualifications to the person who wants to take a better job some time in the future.

ACTIVITY 2

Write out the following sentences, filling in the missing word(s).

1 An aptitude is a natural _____ to do something such as playing games.

2 Manual dexterity means doing something which is _____ with your hands.

3 _____ is important for some leisure jobs if you have to reach things.

4 The ability to keep going without getting too tired is called _____.

5 An employer is likely to be looking for a _____ and tidy person.

6 People who have already had part-time jobs know that they are expected to be _____ and reliable, _____ and polite.

7 When taking a first job, it is a good idea to think where you might _____.

8 Taking advantage of an organisation's _____ courses will help those who want to get a better job in the future.

Personal interests

These are very important for jobs in leisure and tourism, because you will be able to use them in your job or when you are offering help and advice to customers and clients.

Travel agency clerks who have been to the places which customers are thinking about can offer very useful advice and

Personal interests are important for jobs in the leisure and tourism industry.

say if the resort is quiet, lively, suitable for families, couples, teenagers and so on. The sports coach who plays the game for a team will have a useful store of information as well as enthusiasm for the people who are learning to play.

ACTIVITY 3

1 Write down a list of your own personal interests, particularly those which match the last piece of work under the heading: 'Jobs which you think you could do now'.

2 Add to this list your personal qualities, some of which you could take from the list just given in this book. Add any other personal qualities which belong to you.

Experience and achievements

Many students have had training through work experience or held part-time jobs during the Foundation year. These experiences will show that you can arrive on time, follow instructions and do the job; be pleasant to customers, your employer and your fellow workers; and work either in a group or by yourself until the job has been completed. You will also understand about taking care of the health and safety of yourself and others at work and know that if you all pull together, the business will prosper and jobs will be possible.

The achievements you have gained will be personal ones and could include NVQ or GNVQ, GCSEs or computer literacy such as CLAIT (Computer Literacy and Information Technology).

ACTIVITY 4

1 Write down a list of your work experience and achievements to date and discuss these with your tutor.

2 Make any additions or alterations you think necessary after your discussion and keep your copy in a safe place for further reference.

One useful achievement for anyone in the leisure and tourism field is a first-aid certificate. If you do not hold one, think about training and obtaining this.

You may well hold awards, badges or certificates from youth organisations or from your hobbies and interests (such as a life-saving certificate in swimming). These certificates should be of fairly recent origin: your cook badge when you were a Brownie Guide would not be suitable!

Leisure activities

As your probable job will be in the field of leisure activities, your leisure activities may give a useful clue as to the type of work which will suit you!

Many people use the home as a source of leisure activities: watching TV, entertaining friends and relatives, occupying themselves with DIY, gardening, reading, listening to music, looking after pets and cars. Others prefer to go out and socialise in bars, clubs, restaurants, like to visit theatres, cinemas or concert halls. Leisure and sports centres attract customers on a regular basis. Spectator sports have a lot of followers: football is the main spectator sport, but people also watch golf, tennis, cricket, etc.

Local parks, swimming baths, libraries, country houses and gardens are well-used leisure facilities. People have minority interests, such as preserving an old railway line complete with train, or learning old crafts and skills.

Many people spend leisure time running churches, youth organisations, charities and raising money for their project.

Some of these things may remind you of your own leisure activities. You will need to list these on any application form or CV when you apply for a job.

ACTIVITY 5

Work in pairs.

1 Each person makes a list of his or her own leisure activities.

2 Each person discusses the list with his or her partner and checks to make sure that all leisure and recreation activities have been mentioned.

3 Take the lists of personal qualities, personal features, personal interests and experience and achievements gained through work and training, the list of other achievements and leisure activities and use them to word process a short account about yourself.

Keep the information safe to use in a future activity.

Curriculum Vitae

This is a sheet of information about you, your education, qualifications, employment, hobbies and interests, and names and addresses of people who will give you an up-to-date reference.

It should fit on one piece of paper if possible, as employers find it tiring to look through lots of information. See the example on the next page.

A first-aid qualification is useful for your CV.

ACTIVITY 6

Look at the example of the Curriculum Vitae which follows. Word process a similar one adapted for yourself. Have it checked by your tutor *before* you print it. You may need several copies when you apply for jobs.

CURRICULUM VITAE

NAME

Alex Jackson

ADDRESS

149 Taunton Road
Grasscroft
MOSSTOWN
MS1 5JA

TELEPHONE NUMBER

0161 567 1789

DATE OF BIRTH

25 January 1981

EDUCATION

Mosstown College of Further Education
Ashley Road, Mosstown

Mosstown High School
Owl Lane, Mosstown

QUALIFICATIONS

General Certificate of Secondary Education:

English (E)
Drama (C)
Science Double Award (E, E)
Computer Design and Technology (D)
Commerce (F)
Mathematics (F)

GNVQ Foundation in Leisure and Tourism:

I have passed all the external tests and expect to get a Pass or Merit grade.

WORK EXPERIENCE

I delivered evening papers for two years. I did work experience in our local library for two weeks. I now have a Saturday job in MacRanald's where I work at the fast food counter cooking and serving snacks and drinks.

OTHER ACHIEVEMENTS

I have Duke of Edinburgh's Bronze Award and have helped with a project converting an old barn into a riding centre for the disabled.

PERSONAL QUALITIES

I am a reliable and honest person. I can keep working at a job until it is finished. I am friendly and a good communicator. I enjoy working with other people.

PERSONAL INTERESTS

I like most sports and I enjoy walking and camping. I like swimming and have gained survival certificates. At the moment I am taking first-aid training.

LEISURE ACTIVITIES

I belong to the college badminton team and I like visiting friends, listening to music and activity holidays.

REFERENCES

References can be obtained from my college tutor, Mrs Ann Kirby and from The Manager, MacRanald's Fast Foods, 83 The High Street, Tetherton, Mosstown.

ACTIVITY 7

1 Look back at the broad headings under which leisure and tourism jobs can be classified at the beginning of this chapter. Write down the headings containing the kinds of work you might like to do.

2 Look back at your list of personal qualities, personal interests, leisure activities and any work or work experience you have already done. Can you think of any jobs which match these?

When you were carrying out your leisure pursuits and interests, you met staff in the leisure and tourism industries. These people may be prepared to tell you about how to apply for any vacancies in their particular field.

Your course tutor will be notified by the local careers officer of jobs which come into them (e.g. a trainee travel agency clerk for Lunn Poly) and will probably talk to you either in a group at college, or in a personal interview at the careers office, about possible vacancies.

The local job centre will also have jobs from local employers, and staff who will be able to help you to choose a suitable job. They will also telephone the employer for an interview and help in other ways.

Other sources of information include the Human Resources staff in various leisure and tourism industries, or the people involved in school-industry links (who arrange your work experience or visits to their organisation).

You should let all your family, friends, neighbours and other contacts know that you are looking for work in a particular field, as they may be able to put you in touch with people looking for employees.

ACTIVITY 8

Make out a list of:

a possible jobs which would suit you.

b possible contacts together with names, addresses and telephone numbers.

c your plans to get in touch with professional advisers (careers office, etc.).

d local professional job vacancy services (such as an employment agency) which may also provide support staff for leisure and tourism.

e magazines and newspapers which carry job advertisements in the areas you are considering.

Answer in full sentences.

_1_ What kind of job in the leisure and tourism industries matches your own personal qualities, interests or leisure activities?

_2_ Give three sources of information about jobs which you might use when you are ready to look for work.

_3_ In what ways might the local job centre help you to obtain work?

_4_ What skills and qualifications will you be able to offer an employer when you have successfully completed the course?

Many local authorities offer jobs in their own leisure and tourism department and these are usually advertised in the local newspaper on a certain night. This list of jobs is also available from your local library.

Besides this source, jobs can be found:

▶ in your local careers office
▶ in your local job centre
▶ through employment agencies
▶ in specialist magazines such as _Caterer and hotelkeeper_
▶ through information given to college tutors
▶ on vacancy boards outside firms
▶ through friends, relatives and neighbours
▶ on radio and TV – Ceefax and Teletext
▶ by writing to firms and asking if they have any vacancies.

Applying for jobs

It is not enough to send off one or two job applications and hope for the best. People who get jobs are those who stick at it. Some ideas for organising your job-hunt are:

▶ have copies of your CV ready to send off when you see a job
▶ make sure your job application is _one of the first_ – firms may not bother to open later letters if they have enough candidates for a shortlist on the first day after the advertisement
▶ cut out a copy of the advertisement and make a copy of your application; staple them together and keep in a safe place

▶ never send the *original* copy of a reference or testimonial – send a photocopy and take the real one to the interview.

If you follow these guidelines you will be well prepared. Some firms do not ask candidates to come for interview for weeks after an advertisement has appeared. If you fasten your *application* to the original *advertisement*, you can look at both just before you go to the interview. The advertisement will probably tell you about the firm itself – whether it has branches all over the country or if it is a small firm. The heading on the letter inviting you to interview may have the names of the directors on it. Look at the signature on the letter to see if you are being interviewed by the boss!

You will probably attend several interviews before someone offers you a job, so it is important to remember (or to look it up in your file) which job you are being interviewed for!

ACTIVITY 10

1 Look in your local newspaper, or choose from the jobs on the following pages, and find a job you could apply for.

2 Cut out (or photocopy the textbook page and cut out) the advertisement you have chosen and use the details to fill in one of the application forms in the next activity.

Filling in the application form

1 Take a copy of the application form and fill that in first. You are sure to make a mistake, change your mind, decide on a better way of putting something if you try to fill it in straightaway!

2 When you are happy with your first attempt, fill in the original using *black* ink or biro. Write *very* neatly – you want the employer to be able to read what you have put! Make sure you have followed any instructions.

3 Take a photocopy of the filled-in application form and fasten it to the job advertisement or information. You may apply for several jobs at the same time and may not be able to

remember what you put on each form by the time you are called for interview. Keep it somewhere safe.

4 There may be a space for 'Additional information'. You can mention that you are honest, hard-working, strong, reliable, punctual, taking driving lessons, and have a good Record of Achievement from school.

What do the items on the application form mean?

▶ **Surname**   This means your last name or your family name.

▶ **Forename(s)**   Your first name(s), your given or Christian name(s).

▶ **Nationality**   You are British unless you were born out of the Commonwealth.

▶ **Next of kin**   This is usually your nearest relation, such as your Mum or Dad. It could be your spouse, a brother or sister, or anyone close to you. It should be an adult because if you were to have an accident at work, the employer would need to get in touch with your next of kin.

▶ **School(s)**   This means your secondary school(s) (not infant or junior).

▶ **Qualifications**   Any examinations which you have passed.

▶ **Work experience**   Any employment or work experience arranged by your school or college.

▶ **Other achievements**   Certificates from your Record of Achievement or from hobbies such as swimming, first-aid and youth organisation awards.

▶ **Leisure activities**   Whatever you do in your spare time – sports which you play, collecting anything, listening to music, reading, voluntary work, membership of teams or organisations, social activities, home-based hobbies.

Job advertisements

TRAVEL AGENCY TRAINEE

Trainee Travel Agency Clerk wanted. Selection includes a test and an interview. There are no specific qualifications needed but any applicants must be keen with a good general education.

Trainees will have an 8-week induction and day release to obtain ABTA and NVQ qualifications.

They will be placed in local holiday agencies, taking holiday bookings and dealing with varied enquiries.

WAGES: £50.00 per week

40 hours a week, 22 days' holiday

Age: 16–18

Fill in the application form.

CAMPSITE REPRESENTATIVES

UK Camps is a division of UK HOLIDAYS PLC and during the summer we require enthusiastic, hard-working people to help to run our campsites in the UK.

Applicants must be 17 or over, physically fit and have good communication skills. The posts will run from the end of May until the middle of September.

If you wish to take a challenge, fill in the application form and send it off at once.

CITY ART GALLERY

Museum attendant/assistant required

Duties include giving information to members of the public, providing a service in moving artifacts from room to room, as needed, and to be a key-holder.

40-hour week over 7 days with duties on some bank holidays.

Training provided.

Fill in the application form.

AIRLINE CABIN CREW
required by UK HOLIDAYS PLC

Trainee Airline Cabin Crew required to fly for a brand-new airline this summer.

Applicants should be 18–30 years with a minimum height of 5'4" and possess excellent health and good eyesight. Education to GCSE or equivalent is required and work experience in a customer service post would be useful.

There are airline benefits, generous salary and good prospects for the successful applicants.

Fill in the application form.

TICKET ISSUING CLERK

required for UK Coach Company Town Centre Office.

Trainee considered.

Good communication skills, experience not essential as training will be given and there are immediate vacancies after training.

Fill in the application form.

TELESALES EXECUTIVE

LANCASHIRE THEME PARK, PRESTON
can boast stunning entertainment with retail and catering hospitality

A Telesales Executive is needed to be responsible for developing business, working with leads from direct marketing campaigns to sell group visits to LANCASHIRE THEME PARK offering entertainment to suit a wide variety of people.

If you can demonstrate an excellent telephone manner and good persuasive skills we will train you for this post.

Fill in the application form.

CATERING ASSISTANT

required for a busy high quality sandwich bar near the City Centre Monday to Friday only.

Fill in the application form.

HOSTESS

to run busy catering facility in South Meldon. The ideal candidate will have experience in the use of vending machines, but training can be offered to a suitable person. Hours of work are 40 per week, salary £8,800.

Fill in the application form.

TECHNICIAN

required for busy city centre arcade. Must be able to deal with fruit machines, videos and pinball machines.

Circa £10,400

Fill in the application form.

SECOND CHEF required for busy pub in Suffolk for 30-bedroom lodge.

Catering experience and basic food hygiene preparation certificate an advantage. Work must be to a high standard and to a controlled budget.

Position is live in.
Salary negotiable.

Fill in the application form.

FULL-TIME KITCHEN PORTER

in a new Restaurant in Chester City Centre.
Experienced quality staff required.
Training for suitable person would be considered.

Fill in the application form.

CHAMBERMAIDS

required for new Hotel in New Quay. Uniform supplied.

Hours and days will be on a rota system. Experience in hotel work preferred but not essential.

Part-time, mornings only considered.

Fill in the application form.

RECEPTIONIST

needed for permanent position in new hotel. Previous experience in hotel reception preferred or training will be given to a suitable candidate. Good communication skills required to deal with customers and staff. Live-in position. Good rates of pay.

Fill in the application form.

TOURISM AND LEISURE
APPLICATION FORM FOR HOTELS, CATERING AND AMUSEMENT PARKS

SURNAME.. FIRST NAME(S) ....

ADDRESS ....

....

TELEPHONE NUMBER .... POST CODE ....

DATE OF BIRTH............................ PLEASE TICK: ARE YOU MALE?........ FEMALE? ....

MARITAL STATUS................................ NEXT OF KIN ....

NAME AND ADDRESS OF SCHOOL ATTENDED ....

....

EXAMINATIONS PASSED ....

....

....

....

PRESENT JOB ....

PLEASE LIST YOUR WORK SKILLS ....

....

....

FURTHER QUALIFICATIONS ....

....

....

HEALTH: HAVE YOU EVER HAD ANY SERIOUS ILLNESSES OR OPERATIONS?

YES/NO...

IF YES, GIVE DETAILS..

HOW DID YOU HEAR ABOUT THIS JOB? ....

PLEASE TELL US WHY YOU THINK YOU WOULD BE SUITABLE FOR THIS

POSITION: ....

....

....

....

SIGNATURE.. DATE ....

TOURISM AND LEISURE
APPLICATION FORM FOR TRAVEL AGENCIES, TRAVEL STAFF, LOCAL AUTHORITY POSITIONS

SURNAME (MR/MRS/MISS/MS) _____

FIRST NAME(S)_____

ADDRESS _____ NATIONALITY_____

_____

TELEPHONE NUMBER_____ DATE OF BIRTH_____

HAVE YOU ANY DISABILITY?_____

EDUCATION

NAME OF SCHOOL/COLLEGE	DATES From/To	AGE ON LEAVING	EXAMINATIONS PASSED	DATE

OTHER QUALIFICATIONS

INTERESTS – Please list your spare time activities. Include membership of any societies or clubs and whether you have held office.

PREVIOUS WORK EXPERIENCE

NAME/ADDRESSES OF TWO REFEREES

Signature_____ Date _____

Here is some information about the companies which have advertised jobs.

- **Lancashire Theme Park:** 180 acres of beautiful parkland, adventure play areas, family attractions, rich varied wildlife, rides, indoor fun house, children's zoo, snack bar and café, group discounts, school discounts, coach drivers are free of charge and provided with a food and drinks voucher.
- **Catering assistant, hostess, technician:** Leisure and Amusement Facilities – city centre location with catering facility, high quality sandwich bar, amusement arcade, cinema, children's rides, fun factory. Open 16 hours a day. Free admission.
- **Second chef, kitchen porter, chambermaids, receptionist:** The Parkgate Hotel – one of the town's finest hotels situated in the city centre, all bedrooms colour TV, tea/coffee makers, choice of menu, bar snacks available all day, fully licensed bars, entertainment each evening, games and snooker rooms, direct dial telephones, full central heating, lifts and car park. Open all year.
- **Travel agency trainee, campsite representatives, airline cabin crew:** Best Choice Holidays (a department of UK Holidays PLC) including UK Coach Company – owns an airline, travel agencies, a coach company and hotels in the UK and abroad, and a car-hire company: every need of the traveller is catered for within this large international organisation.
- **Museum attendant/assistant:** City Art Gallery – owned by Mosstown City Council and situated in the town centre. Part of a series of art galleries and museums including the Costume Museum, Heritage Centre, Craft Shop and Furniture Museum. Staff are sometimes asked to work at other locations.

ACTIVITY 11

Before you attend the 'mock interview' suggested in Activity 17, look at the details about the organisation you have decided to apply to.

If you are asked 'What do you know about our company?' give some of the information which you have read on this page.

Make sure you read the correct information for the job!

Telephoning for a job application form

1 If you are using a payphone, make sure that you have enough money because you may have to speak to several different people.

2 Write down the telephone number you will ring and the name of the person you wish to speak to.

3 Keep a pen and some paper handy; hold the telephone in the hand you do not use to write with.

4 Introduce yourself: 'My name is Joanne Armstrong: I would like to speak to Mrs Johnson, please.'

5 Have a list of questions ready. Speak clearly and more slowly than you would do normally.

6 Listen carefully and write down any information you are given.

7 You may have to answer questions about yourself.

ACTIVITY 12

Work with a partner and ask your tutor to take part in the following possible telephone conversation asking for an application form.

YOU — My name is . . . (give your own name), may I speak to Mrs Johnson, please?

TUTOR (as switchboard operator) — This is Mosstown Leisure Services; Chris speaking. I'm afraid Mrs Johnson isn't here at the moment; may someone else help you?

YOU — I'm ringing up to ask for an application form for the job of Swimming Pool Attendant.

TUTOR — I'll put you through to someone else.

PARTNER — How may I help you?

YOU — My name is . . . and I'm ringing up to ask for an application form for the job of Swimming Pool Attendant.

PARTNER — Who put you through to me?

YOU — The switchboard operator . . . I really wanted to speak to Mrs Johnson.

PARTNER — She's not here today . . . just a minute, I'll put you back to the switchboard.

TUTOR — How may I help you?

YOU — My name is . . . and I'm trying to get an application form for the job of Swimming Pool Attendant.

TUTOR — There's no-one here to help you . . . can you ring again tomorrow?

It is to be hoped that you don't encounter difficulties like this, but it is true that you sometimes find yourself put through from person to person until you find someone who can help you.

ACTIVITY 13

Re-write the previous telephone conversation with your partner now playing a much more helpful role. If possible, record this new script and then listen to it carefully to see if you could improve it. Keep the tape to use as evidence.

ACTIVITY 14

Fill in an application form (choose the relevant one) for your chosen job. Read the details about how to fill it in that we covered previously.

The interview

1 You will probably receive a letter inviting you to attend for the interview. There will be some details at the top of the letter, such as the name of the firm, the telephone and fax numbers, and possibly other information such as the directors. Look at this letter heading and try to remember the information on it.

2 Find out where the firm is and if possible go there, checking on public transport or car parking facilities.

3 Make sure you arrive on time and take with you the letter asking you to attend, your certificates and any other proof of qualifications. When you get to the firm, there will probably be a reception desk so you should know who to ask for.

4 Dress suitably in comfortable clothes; don't be tempted to go shopping on the way there and arrive carrying several bags! If you feel wind-blown or want to tidy yourself, ask at reception for the cloakroom.

5 *In the interview room*

   Smile, if possible, when you go in and use the interviewer's name if you know it: 'Good morning, Mr Kenning.'

   Don't sit down until you are asked to do *and never smoke.*

Dress as smartly as possible when attending interviews.

Listen carefully to the questions; answer as fully as possible even if you have to pause to think about it. *Never* say just 'Yes' or 'No'.

6 *The hidden interview*

Keep on your best behaviour if you are shown round the premises by someone else. Take an interest in what you are being shown. At the end, thank the interviewer for seeing you.

7 Work out the answers to:

▶ What do you know about our company? (Of course, you have read the details on the letter heading and the job advertisement; asked friends and family what they know about the firm and you have read any brochures left lying in reception.)
▶ What makes you think you could do the job? (You tried it on work experience, it is similar to the work you have done in college, you have done it as a temporary job.)

8 More answers to work out:

▶ What are your hobbies and interests? (You can use the ones you have put on the application form; this question is meant to get you talking.)
▶ What newspaper do you read? (They may expect you to keep up with what is going on in the world. If you don't read a newspaper, perhaps you had better begin. See what they have in your school, college or public library!)
▶ What do you think about the latest ferry (or air, or rail) disaster? (Watch the TV news for a week or so before your interview so that you know the latest news. Again, this can start you talking.)

9 Have some questions ready such as:

▶ Will I be working with people of my own age?
▶ What arrangements are there for lunch?
▶ What are the chances of promotion if I work hard?
▶ Is there any further education or training?
▶ Will I have to work late or do overtime?
▶ Will I have to move round the different centres?

10 More things to say:

Organisations like you to find out that theirs is a steady, reliable, well-known company, recommended by your friends, neighbours and/or relatives as being a good place to work.

---

11 What you don't say:

Don't ask about money, holidays or giving notice – you don't want to sound as if you're only interested in the pay, days off and leaving the firm! These details will be given to you either at the interview or in your Contract of Employment.

Don't make jokes because you are nervous.

12 Remember –

▶ speak up
▶ don't slouch
▶ show that you match the requirements for the job.

The interviewer is hoping that *you* will be the one for the job, then he or she will be able to have a coffee break!

13 Looking well presented:

For the 'mock' interview which follows, dress in your most suitable clothes and then have a photograph taken which you can keep and use to provide evidence for main stages of recruitment.

ACTIVITY 15

Work in small groups of not more than four people.

1 In turn, each person will be interviewed for a job by the other members of the group and the tutor, who plays the part of the Human Resources Officer.

2 Use the job application form you filled out in Activity 14 and make sure the interviewing members know which job you are applying for.

3 Make a list of the people in your group to be interviewed and decide on a suitable room, date and time.

4 Using the list, write out the candidate and the interviewing committee for each interview. For instance, if the group consists of Michael, Susan, John and Lindsay the list would read:

Candidate: Michael   Room D12 at 10.00 am
Interviewing committee: Susan, John, Lindsay, Human Resources Officer.

Candidate: Susan   Room D12 at 10.30 am
Interviewing committee: John, Lindsay, Michael, Human Resources Officer

Candidate: John   Room D12 at 11.15 am
Interviewing committee: Lindsay, Michael, Susan, Human Resources Officer

Candidate: Lindsay   Room D12 at 11.45 am
Interviewing committee: Michael, Susan, John, Human Resources Officer

5 Once the list is ready, a letter is prepared to send to the candidate. The first person named on the interviewing committee sends the letter to the candidate. Word process the letter that follows, using the correct date, times and names (instead of the ones shown in this example). The person who prepares the letter also signs it. Fill in the job which has been applied for.

MOSSTOWN LEISURE CENTRE
Ashley Road
MOSSTOWN

Telephone: 0161 345 6789

Fax: 0161 345 3621

(Put today's date here)

Mr Michael Green
10 Firth Lane
MOSSTOWN

Dear Mr Green

Thank you for your application form for a job as .... at the above Leisure Centre.

We should be glad if you would attend for interview in Room D12 on Friday 28 June at 10.00 am. Please bring this letter with you and ask at the Reception Desk for Room D12.

We look forward to meeting you and to discussing your job application.

Yours sincerely

Susan Bromwell

Susan Bromwell (Miss)

🏃 🏃 🏃 🏃 🏃 **ACTIVITY 16** 🏃 🏃 🏃 🏃 🏃

1 When you receive your letter inviting you to attend the interview, write back and state that you will be coming. Put your own correct details in the following letter and word process it.

2 Keep a copy of the letter you receive and a copy of your reply to it. In a real situation, these would be pinned to your copies of the application form and the job advertisement.

You would also take the letter asking you to attend the interview with you so that the firm knows you have been invited to go there.

You may be given a badge by the receptionist and asked to wear it whilst you are on the premises.

```
                                                                    10 Firth Lane
                                                                    MOSSTOWN
                                                                    M39 3TN

(Put today's date here)

Mosstown Leisure Centre
Ashley Road
MOSSTOWN

For the attention of Miss Susan Bromwell

Dear Sirs

Thank you for your letter inviting me for an interview on Friday 28 June at 10.00 am in Room D12.
I will be attending the interview and look forward to meeting you and finding out more about the job.

Yours faithfully

M. Green

Michael Green
```

You may have noticed two differences as follows.

- The letter to Michael began 'Dear Mr Green' and ended 'Yours sincerely'. This is because the writer used Michael's name. If you begin with a person's name, then 'Yours sincerely' is the ending. Remember if you put the words 'since' and 'rely' together, they spell 'sincerely'.
- The second letter from Michael was marked 'For the attention of Miss Susan Bromwell' because she is the person at the firm who is dealing with this matter. It begins 'Dear Sirs' because it is to the Leisure Centre (not Susan personally – she just works for the Centre) so it must end 'Yours faithfully'.

Both letters have the sender's name *printed* underneath the signature, since some signatures are not very easy to read.

Work in the groups you were in for Activity 15.

1 As a group, work out the questions you will ask the candidate. You may want to give out some questions each to the people on the interviewing committee.

2 The interviews take place as follows.

- ▶ The Human Resources Officer will introduce the members of the committee to the candidate.
- ▶ The members will then ask their questions.
- ▶ The Human Resources Officer will explain about the pay – whether it is weekly or monthly. There will also be some information about the job, such as the hours to be worked, days off, holidays and who the candidate will report to.
- ▶ The candidate will then be asked if he or she has any questions to ask.

- ▶ The Human Resources Officer will then tell the candidate that he or she can expect to hear by the end of next week whether or not he or she has been given the job.
- ▶ The candidate then thanks the committee and leaves the room.
- ▶ The committee should then make notes of all the good points of the candidate.
- ▶ The next candidate is called, the committee re-forms and the next interview takes place.

3 After all the interviews, the group meets again and discusses the good points of each candidate.

It is often very hard to choose a candidate, so things like experience in the job, being able to speak to people easily may sway the committee to one particular person.

Each person writes to his or her own candidate again, saying that:

- ▶ he or she has got the job of (whatever was applied for) and will start at 0900 hours on 1 July next
- ▶ a Contract of Employment is enclosed which should be signed and returned by next Friday

- ▶ the writer looks forward to seeing the person and hopes that he or she will find a satisfactory career with Mosstown Leisure Centre.

Word process the letter, address it correctly and use the correct beginning and ending.

Letter of application

Sometimes you are asked to write a letter of application for a job. Look at the advertisements again and choose one. Adapt the following letter of application so that it is from yourself applying for that job. Use the name and address shown here to send your letter to.

18 Hopedale Way
MOSSTOWN
M3 9GJ

(Put today's date here)

Mosstown Leisure Complex
The Town Centre
MOSSTOWN
M1 3KJ

Dear Sirs

With reference to your advertisement for a receptionist in the new hotel which appeared in the Mosstown Evening News yesterday, I should like to apply for the post.

I have just completed Foundation GNVQ Leisure and Tourism. I have passed all the external tests and expect to obtain a Merit grade. During my year at Mosstown College of Further Education I have also had an evening job as a waitress at Greengate Hotel, Market Street. I have also worked there for a fortnight over the Christmas holiday period, when I took over the reception desk for an hour at lunchtime.

I have had a fortnight's work experience dealing with the public in Dykes Travel Centre, Mosstown, where I used computerised systems to make travel and holiday bookings under the supervision of a qualified travel agent. I enjoyed this work very much and I found that I like talking to and helping people.

I consider myself to be a reliable, hard-working and friendly person. Working with the public is something which I enjoy and I am hoping to find a position similar to the one you have advertised.

I enclose a copy of my curriculum vitae and hope to hear from you.

Yours faithfully

(WORD PROCESS OR TYPE YOUR OWN NAME HERE)

Enc

'Additional information' on the application form

Some application forms have an 'additional information' section for you to fill in.

In this section, you should state clearly why you are interested in the job and give details of any relevant experience you may have had. The second and third paragraphs of the Letter of Application (used for Activity 19) have some ideas which you may like to use.

Try to make this section interesting and give information which will be useful to the person who receives your form.

Write in your neatest handwriting and check your spelling in a dictionary if you are not certain it is correct.

ACTIVITY 20

Imagine that you have now been working for two years in the job you have applied for. You are now ready to progress.

1 Look at the main ways to find out about job vacancies. Use one of these ways to find a job which might be the next step up for you.

2 Write a paragraph stating why you are interested in the job, and what experiences you have had in your present job which would be useful. Remember to check spellings in your dictionary or if you are using word processing, with the spell-check.

3 Keep a copy of this paragraph with other materials that you will use for obtaining a job, e.g. your certificates.

Record of Achievement

Most people have a National Record of Achievement from school which they can add to if they take a year at college.

For your Foundation GNVQ in Leisure and Tourism, add a page as follows:

Curriculum followed (*put the year here*)

GNVQ Level I (Foundation) in Leisure and Tourism

Units:

1. **Providing service to customers.**

2. **Preparing visitor information materials.**

3. **Investigating working in the leisure and tourism industries.**

(*Add here any optional units which you have done during this year*)

CORE SKILLS

1. **Application of number**

2. **Communication**

3. **Information Technology**

(*Add any other courses which you may also be following*)

The following headings and the information given are intended as guidelines for your own Record of Achievement. You will read the guidelines and use or adapt them to your own life.

Word process this information and have it corrected by your tutor *before* you print if possible. This information can then be added to your Record of Achievement as a record of your Foundation year.

CROSS CURRICULAR SKILLS

Personal effectiveness

I am punctual for appointments such as interviews and work experience. I am also punctual for lessons in college.

I have coped well with the requirements of the course and passed the tests in _____. I can start and see through the tasks required with (little) help from others and I can work to a deadline. I have demonstrated this by handing my work in on time.

I can work in a team and identify problems to be solved when doing a given task. I have shown this by producing a Plan of Action before beginning an assignment in order to organise my work.

I discussed problems with my group and with my tutor and I used books, visits, surveys and discussions with my tutor to obtain information. I can choose the best way to do the work and state why other ideas would not work as well. I have shown this in my evaluation of the work.

Economic awareness

I am able to budget for my own requirements (and I have a part-time or a temporary or holiday job). I understand what is required when asked to design something and I worked out costs when designing a leaflet for visitors.

I am aware of the Health and Safety at Work Act in relation to the working environment. (When I did my work experience I looked at information on the organisation's health and safety policy.)

Technology for all

I am aware of the impact of technology on society today. I can use a (washing machine, microwave oven, video recorder, central heating controls, electronic till, laser gun to read prices on barcodes) (Note: add any other information here which refers to you).

Information technology

I can use computing packages, for example (give the name of packages you know). I can also produce databases and spreadsheets and I understand their use. I can evaluate the information technology I use to see if it produces the required result.

Communication skills

I can read and choose information from books. I know the difference between factual information (e.g. a list of opening times at a leisure centre) and opinion (e.g. it always rains in the Lake District).

Written skills

I have demonstrated written skills in my Leisure and Tourism assignments. I wrote part of the questions needed when I took part in a mock interview. I have written an example of a letter of application for a job and my own Curriculum Vitae. I can spell, punctuate and use correct structure and layout in letters, memos and other written material.

Oral skills

I can vary ways of speaking to suit different audiences, such as other members of my group and people in outside organisations. For instance, when the group did mock interviews, I asked questions to suit the role I was playing.

Listening

When we had group discussions, I listened to the points of view from other members of the group. I am able to identify a speaker's attitude and feelings and can listen to fellow students.

General
I am aware of the power of images, symbols and objects in communication and the ways in which these can be used in advertising to persuade people to buy products. I can also understand and respond to non-verbal communication such as body language.

Equal opportunities
I understand the main provisions of the law which forbids racist, sexist and other behaviour which makes distinctions between people.

Numeracy
I can choose and use instruments for making measurements and have completed numeracy assignments on percentages, money, diagrams, estimating and converting and have applied this knowledge to leisure and tourism work. (Note: add any other information here which refers to you.)

Personal and career development
After my present course, I intend to (add information here which refers to you) and I understand how to apply for jobs and further courses.

My interests are (add information here which refers to you).

Student statement
(Note: this is a general statement. You will have to choose the things which apply to you and perhaps add other items yourself.)

I found many things worthwhile about the course. One experience I enjoyed was (add information here which refers to you).

I found that being given an assignment and having to work out a Plan of Action to complete it was different from the way I have worked before. I found the tests (easy, hard, fair).

I feel happy about my achievements on the course and I have gained experience in using the computer. When I leave the course I intend to (add information here which refers to yourself).

I feel that I am a reliable person as I have had ___ % attendance. My health is good and I am usually punctual for lessons. I have made friends with people in the group and I have friends in college (school) and at home. I have good relationships with my family.

At the end of the course, I now feel more confident about my ability to (speak to adults, hold down a job, take another course). My tutors are happy with my work and I have learned to operate as part of a team in order to complete some of the assignments.

Check your own personal Record of Achievement for the Foundation year and either add it to your present, or make a new, Record of Achievement.

Keep this somewhere safe as you may need to show it when you go for a job interview.

Evidence indicator

1 Write a short account of the ways in which you might find out about jobs in travel and tourism. You should mention: job advertisements and where to find them; professional advisers and what you must do to seek information from them; other informed sources (such as radio and TV Ceefax and Teletext, etc.).

2 Write a short account of the way in which you followed the main stages in recruitment from choosing a job advertisement to getting a letter saying that you were a successful applicant.

Include with your account copies of:

▶ the job advertisement
▶ your correctly-completed application form
▶ your letter inviting you to attend for interview
▶ your photograph of yourself when you went for interview
▶ your notes on the answers to interview questions.

Also mention:

▶ whether you felt well prepared or not
▶ any improvements you would make for a real interview
▶ what other information about the job you would like to have been given at the interview.

3 Present copies of:

▶ a second completed application form for a job
▶ a letter of application for a job
▶ your own personal Record of Achievement with information about your further achievements on this course
▶ your CV containing the following personal information:
  – subjects studied and qualifications or awards

- experience and achievements gained through work and training
- other achievements
- personal qualities
- personal interests
- leisure activities.

Write a brief account stating how you would present this personal information to a prospective employer.

Evaluation

1 Look at the work you have completed in this assignment.

2 Write a short account of the good ideas and any ideas which didn't work.

3 How could you improve the way in which you tackled this work?

Revision and specimen test questions

Focus 6: Ways of presenting personal information

Reference: Element 3.3 PC1, PC4

External test requirements

a *Identify different ways of presenting personal information to prospective employers.*

Range

Ways of presenting: letter of application, application form, CV, Record of Achievement

Many organisations ask job applicants to send for an application form which has to be filled in and sent back. It is useful to take a copy and fill that in first, in case mistakes are made, and then fill in the actual form. Letters of application can be studied and then adapted to the particular job advertised. Copies of a CV can be made and kept on hand to save time when applying for posts. A Record of Achievement should be brought up to date with your present year of activity.

1 Students may send out several letters of application for different jobs at the same time. To save re-writing the same information about themselves in each letter, they may enclose their:

a Record of Achievement folder
b GCSE certificates
c provisional driving licence
d Curriculum Vitae (CV)

2 Look at the first advertisement below which appeared in the local paper.

Which one of the following ways should a student present personal information for this particular job?
a send a CV
b fill in an application form
c write a letter
d telephone Customer Services Department

External test requirements

b *Identify personal information which should be included in a given CV.*

Range

Personal information: subjects studied, qualifications/awards, personal qualities, personal interests, experience and achievements gained through work and training, other achievements, leisure activities

Your prospective employer is hoping that you will be right for the job and that too much time need not be spent interviewing unsuitable people. It is useful to give as much personal information as possible on a CV whilst making sure it only runs to one or two pages – a very long CV is felt to be too much to work through.

3 Look at the next job advertisement which appeared in the local paper.

Which two of the following items on a CV would be the most likely reason for choosing someone to interview for the above job?
1 Saturday job experience in another leisure centre
2 GCSE Grade C in Drama
3 work experience in a library
4 life-saving certificate from R.L.S.S.

Choose from:
a 1 and 2
b 2 and 3
c 3 and 4
d 1 and 4

FEMALE AVIATION SECURITY OFFICERS

Several officers are required at Brydon Airport. For reasons of decency, only female applicants are required. (Sex Discrimination Act 1975 Section 72B.)

Applicants are required to deal with people in a pleasant manner whilst carrying out frisking and following required procedures.

Application forms and a job pack available from:

Customer Services Department, Brydon Airport, BRYDON.

RECREATION ASSISTANT WANTED FOR BRYDON LEISURE CENTRE

to carry out duties involving booking the Leisure Hall, getting out and putting away equipment, cleaning and tidying the Hall, changing rooms and cafeteria. Work is usually in the evenings and at weekends and there is the possibility of a job share.

Applicants should be physically fit and preferably possess the R.L.S.S. life-saving certificate as there may be additional duties at the swimming pool.

Telephone 0121 384 6873 for an application form.

Focus 7: Recruitment

Reference: Element 3.3 PC2, PC3

External test requirements

a *Recognise the main ways to find out about job vacancies.*

Range

Main ways to find out: advertisements, professional advisers, other informed sources

Advertisements appear in the press, in trade journals and sometimes on the notice board of the organisation itself. Professional advisers include careers officers, job centre officials, course tutors. Other informed sources can be people who work in an organisation and hear about vacancies, relatives, neighbours, acquaintances and friends who pass information on.

4 One of the main ways to find out about job vacancies in leisure is to:
   a ask passers-by if they know of any leisure jobs
   b wait for someone to make contact

   c watch for jobs advertised in the local paper
   d read career books about leisure pursuits

5 The *first* step in the main stages of recruitment in leisure and tourism is most likely to be:
   a tell your tutor you are thinking of taking a job
   b make yourself available for a squash tournament
   c ask relatives to recommend you some time
   d answer a specific job advertisement

6 When applying for a job, candidates should make sure they have first obtained:
   a the right qualifications
   b the correct uniform
   c personal information about the other candidates
   d a letter from their course tutor

7 The successful candidate for a job will receive a:
   a reference from the careers adviser
   b letter of appointment from the interviewer
   c notice about voluntary activities from the job centre
   d home visit from the managing director

Answer page for external tests

Unit 1

Element 1.1
1 c
2 d
3 b
4 a
5 c
6 b
7 d
8 a
9 a
10 b
11 c
12 c
13 b
14 b
15 d
16 c
17 d
18 b
19 c
20 c
21 a
22 a
23 d
24 b
25 b
26 d
27 b
28 c
29 d
30 a
31 c

Element 1.2
1 b

2 d
3 b
4 b
5 d
6 b
7 a
8 c
9 b
10 d
11 d
12 d
13 c
14 c
15 b
16 a
17 d
18 c

Element 1.3
4 c
5 a
6 b

Unit 2

Element 2.1
1 c
2 d
3 b
4 d
5 d
6 c
7 b
8 c
9 d

10 c
11 a
12 b
13 c

Element 2.2
1 d
2 b
3 a
4 c
5 b
6 c
7 b
8 d
9 c

Element 2.3
1 b
2 d
3 a
4 a
5 c

Unit 3

Element 3.1
1 c
2 a
3 a
4 c
5 b
6 c
7 c
8 b
9 b

10 d
11 c
12 b
13 c
14 d
15 b
16 d
17 d
18 a

Element 3.2
1 d
2 b
3 c
4 d
5 c
6 a
7 b
8 b
9 c
10 c
11 a
12 d
13 b
14 d
15 a
16 c
17 d

Element 3.3
1 d
2 b
3 d
4 c
5 d
6 a
7 b

Index